Managing Smaller Projects

•

a practical guide

Managing Smaller Projects
•
a practical guide

Mike Watson

Project Manager Today

Project Manager Today

Published by Project Manager Today Publications
Larchdrift Projects Ltd.
PO Box 55, Wokingham, RG40 4XN

First published in Great Britain 1998

© The Projects Group plc 1998

ISBN 1 900391 02 3

Printed in Great Britain by Digiprint

All authors go through highs and lows. I want to thank both Adrian Dooley of The Projects Group plc for pushing me through the lows and my wife Hannah for helping me enjoy the highs.

Contents

Foreword

This book is all about helping people to control small projects in a logical and effective way, without incurring the high overheads that come with the project management methods, tools and techniques that are now being used so effectively on large projects and within large organisations.

The Small Projects Method (SPM) is designed for use both by complete newcomers to project management and those with some experience. It is logical and practical so that it can be applied to a single, small project, or to a portfolio of many small projects within an organisation.

The danger, especially in larger organisations, is that small projects are left to their own devices while ignoring the fact that together they may represent a significant financial risk that is not being effectively controlled. The only safe and effective way of controlling such activities is to apply the principles of project management.

This book takes those basic principles and gives you the basis for your own project control system.

Mike Watson

Introduction

Many of the methods and techniques used in traditional project management look like proverbial sledgehammers when directed at small projects. So I set out to devise a system that can be used easily to create a way of controlling small projects in any environment. The result is the Small Projects Method (SPM) which is the basis of this book.

I hesitated to call it SPM because it sounds bureaucratic and SPM is nothing of the kind. It is designed to make the adoption of the principles of project management as simple as possible. So here you will find:

- the what, why and how of managing small projects
- a series of standard copyright free forms which you can use, copy or adapt to suit your own environment (see Appendix A)
- checklists to remind you of the various techniques you could apply at each stage of a project (see Appendix B)

In addition to essential background information, the examples and case studies show how you can begin to take control of your projects right away.

I have deliberately left out topics which are interesting and important in the wider context of project management, but are luxuries in dealing with small projects. Hence you will not find such topics as:

- team building and motivation

- personnel management
- meetings
- fact finding
- creativity and decision making
- resolving conflict

Also, because the dividing line between 'small' and 'large' projects is unclear, I have sometimes referred to how a technique might be applied in a 'larger project' without giving further details. This is deliberate as SPM is not designed to be all things to all project managers.

The standard forms included in the text and reproduced in Appendix A are yours to use as you wish; there are also two checklists in Appendix B to remind you of the techniques you should consider at each stage of a project.

I believe that the benefits of adopting the approach given in this book are immeasurable. Use it on your small projects and see the difference. But don't take my word for it, read on and form your own judgement.

Chapter 1

Introducing SPM

Defining a project

The problem is that the word 'Project' is too readily attached these days to activities that are nothing of the kind. We need to establish a definition of a project and its characteristics in order to test any activity to see if it really is a project.

Let's start by defining a project. It is 'the process of carrying out work to achieve a clear objective, usually bringing about change.' This is not very precise, so let's list the usual characteristics of a project:

- agreed, well defined objectives and end products
- a startpoint and an endpoint
- a balance between time, cost and quality
- many interrelated tasks, often grouped into phases
- temporary project team brought together for the project
- multi-disciplinary team
- involvement of people from other organisations
- brings about change

These are projects −

- Moving the office to new premises across town
- Creating the company stand at an exhibition

- Creating a name and address system for marketing mailshots
- Organising the Olympics in Sydney in year 2000
- Building a bridge over a river
- Taking the family on a holiday

These all have the characteristics of projects.

These are not projects —

- Running the office reception desk
- Fixing wheel nuts onto a Ford Mondeo
- Producing the month end accounts

These activities are careful repetitions of a standardised process. They are not projects. Many people confuse the performance of routine tasks with projects; in theory there can be a fuzzy dividing line.

However for all practical purposes if a job consists of carrying out a well-established set of tasks, in an environment that is well understood and stable, with personnel who are trained and experienced in those tasks, then that job is a routine process. It is not a project. As soon as the set of tasks starts to vary from the standard, or the environment takes on an unclear, or unstable aspect, you may be looking at a 'project'.

Signs of a successful project

How do you recognise a successful project? If you could put a 'Yes' against every one of the following characteristics you would be looking at a successful project:

yes?	
yes	it met it's business objectives
yes	it delivered it's end product on time
yes	it delivered it's end product within budget
yes	it's end product met all it's quality criteria
yes	the customer was happy with the end product
yes	the customer uses the end product
yes	the customer wants us to do more
yes	the project team felt good about it
yes	change during the project was managed effectively

In practice, however, there are distressingly few projects that score a 'Yes' against every point.

Sales Manager	Project Manager
routine, from year to year	role ends when project ends
no specific dates other than, say month end	start date, end date difficult to predict
stable organisation	temporary project team
needs set of specialist skills	many different skills needed in team
annual budget easily identified	costs very dificult to estimate
work is repetitive and well-known	work often not done before
room to plan within annual budget	time, cost and quality constraints

Management skills

We need to round off this discussion of definitions by looking at the skills of project management. Compare the working environment of two managers: a project manager and a line manager (say, the manager of the sales department). There are some interesting differences (see above).

You can see that the skills and techniques needed by the project manager are different from those needed by the sales manager. This guide is aimed at putting those skills and techniques into a practical framework so that the project manager improves his or her chances of success.

The need for SPM

As a patient being prepared for minor surgery in a hospital operating theatre you would be rather surprised if the medical team called for a brain scan, full DNA typing, and a test for colour-blindness, before removing your appendix. Interesting and valuable though these tests might be, they would be irrelevant for such a small job. An experienced medical team would know that they might need only to monitor vital and relevant indicators; a novice team might not know which are the vital indicators and which are distractions. The result could be an operation which takes three times as long at four times the cost. Project managers often face similar choices

Imagine your reaction if your boss announces that your company has won the contract to organise the Sydney Olympics in the year 2000.

Terror and panic might be your first reaction, but for a project the size of Sydney 2000 you would find many project management methodologies (standardised approaches), techniques, training courses, consultancy firms and software planning tools all geared up to help you. You would immediately recognise that you were faced with the medical equivalent of transplant surgery and would act accordingly.

Now imagine your reaction to the boss saying: 'I think we should have a stand at the trade exhibition in Harrogate next month, and I want you to organise it'. Your reaction could be one of excitement, or concern, or minor panic, but without some guidelines you might try to manage the exhibition project with the same approach as Sydney 2000. If this happens there are only three possible outcomes. Firstly, you will drown in a sea of overheads; secondly you will give up project management in order to try to get the work done; or, thirdly you will run over budget, work late into the night, and produce a poor end product.

Choosing the right tools

Sorting out the vital few from the trivial many is the prime aim of the small projects method (SPM). Its aim is to combine elements of a full blown project management methodology and the simplicity of the back of an envelope. SPM focuses on the vital few elements, to the exclusion of the techniques that are appropriate only to larger projects.

A few forms are used to document the vital features of a project. These forms must be kept as simple as possible or else you would not bother using them. A complete set of forms is included in Appendix A. There is no copyright on them, so you can copy them, amend them, or ignore them as you see fit! You can also get copies from the *Project Manager Today* website.

Other approaches

For large projects there are any number of methods that you can choose to use (see Appendix C).

Chapter 2

Project Initiation

You are ready to begin your project and need to get it off to a good start. This chapter goes through the steps involved.

Most business life is concerned with judgements or trade-offs, weighing up a range of possible projects and selecting one to start. There are numerous techniques for making the 'right' decision, but these are outside the scope of SPM; SPM starts once the decision to initiate a project has been made.

Even on the smallest project, the project manager would be foolish and irresponsible to spring into action as soon as the starting gun is fired. A few minutes thought at this stage will save a lot of heartache. But what do you need to think about? If the project has some unusual characteristics, what can be done with that information?

The first step in any project is to make time to think and to gain a clearer view of the project based on the conclusions.

Strategic project factors

Firstly, think about the Strategic Project Factors. These sound rather grand, but are simply questions addressing specific issues that must be asked at the start of a project so that the strategy for dealing with the project can be identified. Strategy, in this context, simply means the practical approach you will adopt to tackle the project.

The Strategic Factors are listed below. It may well be that no answers are forthcoming. Some of the questions may be too difficult to answer at the outset, so a mechanism must be created to accumulate useful knowledge for a better answer later. For example, an accurate answer to 'How much will it cost?' may have to be deferred until more research has been carried out.

Problems arising during the project are likely to stem from not having asked the questions; the mere act of asking them can draw attention to just how much is unknown, or unclear, about the project.

Once the questions have been asked (and answered as best you can) you will then be in a better position to decide how to approach the project. The Strategic Project Factors are laid out as a series of questions, in eleven groups.

1. Time Constraints

- Is there a fixed target date?
- How fixed is it? (Is it really fixed, say, by a change in the law, or is it linked to an unmissable business opportunity, or is someone just trying it on?)
- Who fixed it?
- Are there any other intermediate target dates that must be met?
- Is there a particular start date that must be taken into account?
- Are the time deadlines of a lesser priority than something else (e.g. cost)?
- What else?
- Can a phased implementation be considered? (for example can you finish part of the job by the target date, and clear up the rest later?)

2. Project Profile

- Is the reputation of the company, division, management, project manager, team, at stake?
- Who will get to hear about this project?
- Will a failure be public, or is this a simple 'back room' project?
- Will the project be accompanied by publicity, either internal to the company, or in the trade press, or on international satellite television?
- Is there likely to be high-level management interest in this project?
- What will they want to see?
- Will something have to be finished early in order to show success?

3. Costs and Benefits

- Has a cost/benefit analysis been carried out? By whom? When? On what basis? Can the project team see it?

• Has anyone attempted to establish costs? How was this done? Do we have to stick to them? Were the assumptions written down? Can we see them?

• Does this project have a payoff? Who said so? On what basis were possible benefit figures established? How can they be measured?

• What are the relative importance of development costs (i.e. project costs) and the costs of using the end product on an ongoing basis? (Is a quick and cheap solution OK, even if it costs a fortune to use, run, maintain, service?)

4. Business Risk

• How badly will the organisation suffer if this project fails, or if the end product fails to live up to expectations? Will the company go bust?

• What could you lose if the project fails? Customers, sales, staff, money?

• Do you need to keep any aspects of this project secret or confidential (from competitors, staff, etc.)? What would happen if they were to find out what we are doing?

• Do you need to involve Legal, Personnel, Staff Counselling, Accounts, Auditors, outside Statutory or Regulatory bodies?

5. Scope of the Project

• How big is this project? Measured how – people involved, departments affected, locations, outside suppliers? How far apart are these people?

• Will the project have to link with other projects? How and when?

• Will the end product have to link with other products being produced elsewhere? Inside the company, or outside?

6. Project Background

• Is this a totally new business area for the project team? For the organisation?

• Have we done similar things in the past? What happened?

• Are we taking over something that has already been started? Why?

7. Requirements

• Is what we should produce well understood, agreed and stable – especially, will the requirements change during the lifetime of the project?

• Are the requirements designed to be flexible, or are they firm and unchangeable?

• Are these requirements written down? Can the project team see them? Will the project team understand them, or are they very technical?

- Will you have to produce a 'prototype' to help identify and understand the requirements?
- How will the prototype be judged?
- Have the requirements been accepted?

8. Involvement

- Is there commitment at high level for this project? How do we know?
- Will resources be made available to help with the project?
- Will they be appropriately skilled, with appropriate authority to make project decisions?
- Do these resources know about this project?
- What other commitments do they have?
- What are the relative priorities?
- How much time can we expect from them?

9. Technology

- Is the technology in place in our organisation right now, with skilled personnel, documentation etc.? If not, when will it arrive in relation to the rest of the project?
- Is a specification available? Can we use something else as a fallback?
- How many suppliers are involved?
- Who will connect the components together?
- Are the components fully compatible?
- How reliable will the technology be? How reliable must it be? Can the reliability be established?
- Will the project team or the eventual users require training in this technology? How will this be done?
- Will the installation of the technology require other changes or installations (new premises, new furniture, new security, new safety measures)?
- Will the delivery of the technological components cause disruption? Are there personnel or union implications?

10. Project Team

- How likely is it that the project team will be able to give the necessary time to the project? What else will suffer as a result?
- Will the project require new skills or disciplines? How will this need be met?
- Will recruitment take place, or will sub-contractors or outside suppliers be engaged? Who will control these people?

- What are the training requirements for the project team?
- What other resources might be needed (for example, desks, work benches, travel services, temporary accommodation)?

11. Project Management

- How will the project be managed? Will there be regular meetings, reports, presentations?
- Is the project manager experienced, trained, available? What can be done to assist the project manager?
- What standards, guidelines, quality systems, and so on must be followed on this project? If any company standards are not to be followed, why not? Has this been agreed?
- Will any particular techniques be used to manage this project (e.g. SPM)? What effect might this have on the project management overheads?

Using the Answers

Once as many answers as possible have been obtained, it might be tempting to dive in and start work. You would certainly be in a stronger position than before, but you must now consider the supreme question of all: 'So What?'.

OK, so you discover that the technology you depend upon will not be delivered until half way through the project: So what? Does it matter, and if so, in what way? Asking the questions is straightforward. What you do about the answers may stretch your experience, imagination, and general resourcefulness.

So, maybe you could plan to use some other type of technology early in the project, and only rely upon the newer stuff when it arrives later on; or you could build in an allowance for overtime working in the second half of the project; or you could find someone else who already has the newer stuff, and try to do some of your work at their premises; or you could. . . If you know in advance, you can run the project accordingly; if you are caught out later, you will be reacting to the project, not managing it.

By bringing all these 'strategic' factors out into the open before the project gets under way you can accomplish two key tasks. Firstly, you can document and communicate to all parties the true state of the conditions surrounding the project. Secondly, you can build your project plan taking the conditions into account.

Let us start the planning process, based upon the Strategic Factors.

Developing a Strategy

The point of having a strategy is to see the project in its wider context and to be able to see a way of tackling it.

Any large problem, when broken down into smaller, more manageable pieces, suddenly loses its mystery. If the breakdown into smaller pieces is based upon an organised set of questions (the strategic project factors), then the project suddenly looks possible and much less daunting.

Phases

The outcome of the Strategic Factors exercise is a list of project pieces. Actually, these 'pieces' have a wide range of names. Most people use terms such as 'phases', 'stages', or even 'chunks'. I shall use the word 'phase' to describe a piece of a project.

While on the topic of jargon, I shall call the process of breaking a project down into manageable pieces 'structuring' (our American cousins use the term 'Chunking' — an unappealing word, but very descriptive of the process!).

Examples

Here are some examples of using the strategic factors to carry out 'structuring'.

Project 1: 'Move our office 2 miles across town'

The Strategic Factors questions uncovered the following project characteristics:

1. Date Constraint:
the old office will be handed back to the landlord on 31st October; we HAVE to be out by that date.

2. Date Constraint:
we can gain access to the new office on 1st October, but only for decorating and wiring; we cannot move furniture in until 15th Oct.

3. Business Risk:
October is one of our busiest months for sales calls and we cannot afford to lose any.

4. Background:

the telephone company messed us around the last time we moved.

5. Technology:

we will take the opportunity to install a new state-of-the-art computer network for all administration.

Strategy

What must we do to take this information into account when planning *Project 1*? Some suggestions include:

1. Sales Dept. must be the top priority; they should be moved first.

2. Yes, install the new network wiring and so on, but let's settle in with the old systems; we can finish the network job after the move (i.e. a two phase approach).

3. We should investigate using alternative phones, for example mobiles, to tide us over during the difficult period (contingency).

This powerful principle of asking the questions and acting upon the facts, increases the chances of success. From these answers the details emerge. So, the outline sets of phases for *Project 1* could look like this:

1. Basic decoration
2. Install network and other wiring
3. Set up contingency sales dept.
4. Move In
5. Install new network system

What is emerging is the general outline of a plan for the project. At this stage, this level of detail is sufficient. Sometimes you must resist very strongly the temptation to dive too deeply into detail.

Documenting the project

You do need to write this down in some form. You will be questioned about the project and you should be very sure of your ground before initiating any project tasks.

Project definition

This is the time to introduce form SPM1— the SPM Project Definition Form. **In most cases, this will be the only formal documentation necessary for a small project.** On occasions where a project may need slightly more documentation, then extensions to SPM1 can be used. As you progress through this book, following the stages of setting up and executing a project, the relevant parts of SPM1 will be completed. Right now, at the project initiation stage, begin the process of writing down what you believe the project is, and how you intend to tackle it. This all fits on SPM1. A complete set of blank forms is included in Appendix A.

First, the easy bits. Fill in the project name and brief description This may be a snappy name that people will remember and help easily identify the project. You can then fill in the sections based upon answers to the Strategic Factors questions.

Objectives

The Objectives of the project should be entered before anything else. They describe what it is all about. Also, priorities may come into play and this is where we can state them. Objectives should be **SMART**:

S	Stated Clearly, so there is no argument
M	Measurable, so you know when to stop
A	Agreed, by all parties, in advance
R	Realistic, and prioritised
T	Time-related, to give time targets

Here are some examples: The objectives of *Project 1* (Office Move), could be:

- to move the entire contents of the office from Location A to Location B
- not to lose a single Sales Enquiry while moving
- to install a new network system
- installation of the new network is a lower priority than maintaining a full sales service

Once the Objectives have been agreed and written on SPM1, they form a base from which the project can be managed.

If the objectives change during the course of the project then they can be re-visited, amended and re-agreed. Think of them as forming part of a contract between the Project Sponsor and the Project Manager (don't worry about these terms, more about them in Chapter 3).

The Objectives are the underlying basis of the project, but can always be changed, with agreement.

Scope

The Scope of the project is the next item to document. Again, based upon the answers to the Strategic Factors questions, you can now specify what is included in the project, and almost more importantly, what is NOT included.

Scope describes parts of the organisation, or geographical areas, or branches of the business, or whatever. It's the scope that provides the boundary around the project.

> **• Project 1 Scope might be:**
> The move includes all office equipment, furniture, shelves, and staff, but excludes carpets, blinds, telephone system.

> **• Project 2 Scope (Company stand at an exhibition) might be:**
> The project must include design and production of all exhibition give-aways, staff travel and accommodation, and a sales leads follow up system, but does not include buying the stand or any of the fittings, as these will be supplied by the Exhibition Organisers.

Defining the scope is essential. By establishing agreement to the scope at the initiation stage you can reduce the chance of disappointment at the end of the project when people don't get what they expected.

Again, an agreed scope at the outset gives you a base to return to if you discover that the scope needs changing; unmanaged creeping scope is the bane of all project managers.

Constraints

Next on the list are the constraints on the project. Traditionally, constraints include time (start dates, end dates, seasonal considerations), resources (availability and skill levels of people), budget, methods and rules that have to be followed and so on. The constraints for *Project 1* might include:

- We must be out of the old office by 31st Oct.
- We cannot get into the new office until 1st October, and, even then, we cannot move furniture in until 15th Oct.
- October is the busy season for sales

The constraints for *Project 2* (Exhibition Stand) might include:

- Give-aways must be produced three days before exhibition, for shipping
- Budget limit is £1500
- All give-aways must conform to the new corporate image standards

Documenting constraints is vital but must never be allowed to turn into a back-covering exercise. The project cannot be planned or managed without a clear statement of the constraints. If the project has to change shape later during its life the constraints may need to be reviewed (for example, a date might be relaxed, or more money found to overcome a problem). Without the initial agreement on constraints, all subsequent actions can be rather reactive, with no mechanism for understanding the consequences of changing a constraint.

Roles and Responsibilities
This section deserves its own chapter and is dealt with next.

Main Products/Deliverables
At this stage it is also important to establish and agree exactly what is to be produced by the project and, where necessary, agree on the format.

All projects produce something tangible, and the Main Products/ Deliverables section on SPM1 is the place to state what the project is designed to produce. The end product (many people use the term deliverable; the terms are interchangeable) and, to some extent, the intermediate products can often be a source of confusion and misunderstanding. So the better they can be defined at the outset the more chance of success.

Many projects produce 'only' a report; state what the report is to be used for and, if known at this stage, list the major topics to be covered by the report. The principle behind this section of SPM1 is to avoid the surprise at the end of the project, when the sponsor gets something they didn't expect.

If there are company or legal standards to be followed, this can be stated here to clarify the nature of the product. If the product is to be the subject of a series of stringent quality checks, these can be spelt out in more detail on the Project Quality Plan form, which is described in Chapter 8.

An example for the Office Move Project might include a technical specification of the new network, including performance and resilience characteristics. This definition will give the technical members of the project team a clear target at which to aim.

External dependencies

The section to complete at this stage also uses information straight out of the strategic factors questions. Very few projects nowadays take place in isolation; most organisations have several (even many) projects under way at any one time. In many cases these projects interact with each other.

The external dependencies section of SPM1 is the place where you can take note of the way that other projects will influence your project. Such information is vital in the planning process.

For example, the external influences section for *Project 1 (Office Move)*, might include:

> • there is a company project looking into the new Health & Safety Regs. as they apply to users of computers

The external influences section for *Project 2 (Exhibition Stand)*, might include:

> • the annual company conference is taking place the previous week. All publishing and graphics staff are fully allocated to preparing materials for that

External Influences for *Project 3 (new Mailing Database)*, might include:

> • the Boss has just initiated a project to look at buying Name and Address lists from third parties, and these might need to be incorporated into our future name and address system

Assumptions

It is often impossible to bring all the project characteristics out into the open. Sometimes, because of a lack of time, or knowledge, you have to guess the key factors. There is nothing wrong with guessing, as long as two other precautions are taken.

First, write down the guesses in the underlying assumptions section of SPM1. This at least shows that they are assumptions, not facts.

Second, put some actions into play that are designed to clear up the assumptions at the earliest opportunity. These actions may form an early phase of the project (many engineering prototypes are built in order to clear up assumptions about the end product). Then reshape the project based upon the information you glean from these actions.

Phases/Tasks

Based upon the structuring exercise, the Phases can be documented. If the project is really small then the Phases list may be all that is needed. Usually, however, a slightly more detailed project plan is required (more of this in Chapter 4). In this latter case the Phase list from SPM1 becomes essential input to the planning process in which the phase can be broken down into more detailed tasks.

However, for very small projects the Phase list is enough. Just put down the phase names at present. Resources and dates will be filled in later.

Outline Plan

As a result of asking the Strategic Factors questions and then taking a critical look at the answers, you will know quite a bit more about the project. You can see what it consists of, what the objectives are and the major constraints. You also have an outline plan (for that is what the Phase list is) showing how you intend to tackle the project.

You have also started the process of documenting the project in a simple manner, using SPM1, the project definition form.

There are several more sections of this form that must be completed at the Project Initiation stage. The next is roles and responsibilities.

/

Chapter 3

Roles and Responsibilities

It is important to get a clear definition of certain key roles in a project, and there is a simple approach to the question: 'Who is responsible for this?'

Jobs versus roles

A common approach to managing projects — especially smaller projects — is to appoint a skilled and experienced person to the ROLE of project manager. Often this appointment lasts only for the duration of the project. At the completion of the project, the person returns to their previous duties.

It might not be ideal, but very often the role is part-time, with the project manager having to achieve project objectives while holding down a routine job within the organisation.

It is also common nowadays for the project manager not to be the line manager of the project team. In fact, the project team itself may be a disparate mix of skilled individuals put together for the duration of the project.

None of these combinations matter much, as long as the roles and responsibilities are defined and understood at the outset.

Three main roles need to be given on SPM1, the project definition form. The roles are 'Project Customer', 'Project Sponsor', and 'Project

Manager'. Not every project will require people to be assigned to all three.

Finding the customer

The person who asked you to undertake the project may also be the person who will use and benefit from the end product the thing the project produces. It is more common, however, to find that the 'customer' is not the person who assigned you the project. This introduces the possibility of a divergence of views between the person who commissioned the project and the final user. For example, the Marketing Director, who initiated the exhibition stand project, may have a different vision from the senior sales person who will run the stand. Get the roles and responsibilities out into the open at the start (instead of at the exhibition!). This will nip problems in the bud.

The term used to describe the person who benefits from the project is the 'Project Customer'. There may be a large number of apparent customers, but there is usually one representative who can be called the 'Customer'.

Examples

For example, the Project Customer for *Project 1, Office Move,* is the supervisor of the office being moved. This is the person who will benefit from the move and will have to use the new setup.

The Project Customer of *Project 2, the Exhibition Stand,* is the senior sales person who will be running the stand.

The Project Customer of *Project 3, the new name and address system,* is the section leader who is responsible for maintaining the name and address database.

Why do we need one?

It is important to identify the customer for the following reasons:

- It is the customer who will use the end product, so it ought to be the customer who has a major input to the scope, objectives and constraints

- Most projects require the active support and commitment of the customer for the whole duration of the project to have any chance of success

The customer's views and judgement will be vital if project priorities need to be reviewed and changed. Any arbitrary change to the main project aims made by the project team, with no reference to the customer, will whittle away at the customer's commitment to the project.

The customer may be required to supply key resources to the project, albeit only part-time. These resources will probably also have to carry out their regular duties while helping on the project, so commitment to the project by all concerned is essential.

Early identification and involvement of the customer is valuable. However, just pointing the finger at someone and saying 'congratulations, you are the Project Customer', is not enough! If you cannot tell them what their role is expected to be, then you do not deserve their support. So, think about the likely elements in the role of a Project Customer:

• providing advice and input to the initiation stage, when Objectives, Scope and Constraints are agreed

• providing skilled and experienced resources to assist the project teams

• contributing to decision-making concerning project progress, rescheduling etc.

• informing the project team of quality issues, changing business requirements etc.

• testing, or trying out, things produced by the project team, and advising on their acceptability

• accepting the final end product

It is unlikely that the customer's role will be full time, although it may well extend over the duration of the project. The Project Manager, when negotiating with the Project Customer's commitment, must be prepared to indicate just how much involvement will be needed and its timing. This can best be confirmed when the project plan begins to emerge.

The other important aspect of this role is that of authority. A small, quick moving project should not be held up because the Project

Customer's representative does not have the authority to approve a key project item. Again, when the plan has emerged in more detail the scope and nature of the necessary authority can be identified.

The Project Sponsor

The concept of a Project Sponsor is commonplace, but many people, Sponsors included, have no formal knowledge of the role and its attendant responsibilities. This can lead to sponsors laying down the law about 'their project' with no idea of the consequences, or implications, of their actions.

As the Sponsor's role is so important, you must make sure you understand why one is needed and what the Sponsor should be responsible for.

The Sponsor is one of the main decision-makers on the project. He or she is the 'champion' of the project when decisions about the project's interface with the business environment must be made. For example, if the project starts to slip against budget, the sponsor may have to go 'into battle' to obtain approval for more expenditure.

Examples

Likely Sponsors for our sample projects might be:

- Project 1, Office Move: *Premises Manager*
- Project 2, Exhibition Stand: *Marketing Director*
- Project 3, New Database: *Marketing Director*

You can see from these limited examples that senior management can collect many project sponsorships. They may find the idea of being a Project Sponsor quite attractive if they are unaware of the detailed responsibilities. It is very important to spell out the role of Sponsor before you ask someone to take it on. They have to realise that this is more than a figurehead role.

The role of the Project Sponsor

The detailed responsibilities of a Project Sponsor include:

- to approve the project plans (and by this I mean all aspects of project initiation)
- to agree and deliver necessary resources

- to monitor progress via the project manager
- to ensure quality via the project customer
- to resolve project-business conflicts (especially in the areas of budget and resources)

It is clear from this list that the role of Project Sponsor is not full time, but may involve intense activity from time to time. **A prospective sponsor must understand this commitment before agreeing to take on the role.**

In many instances, the Sponsor does not 'take on' the role, because the sponsor is the initiator of the project. However, even in these cases, it is important for the sponsor to understand the responsibilities associated with 'dishing out' a project. It is all too easy to feel very dynamic when you cause lots of people to scamper about while forgetting that responsibility is two-sided. When a project begins to run into trouble the project sponsor has a key role to play in steering it back on course. This may be time-consuming and full of hassle; but it will be a major factor in the eventual successful outcome of the project.

The project manager

In its simplest form the responsibility of the Project Manager is to ensure that the project is successful. This means producing the required end products to the required quality standard, within the specified constraints of time and cost.

Why do we need one?

If the project team knows what to do, why do we need a Project Manager? Well, how did the team come into being, and how do they all know what to do? Who told them? Who will keep the project rolling along even when the world outside the project is changing rapidly? Who will the Sponsor seek out for progress information?

Some organisations run on democratic lines, with no 'boss'. This can work well, but a project can cut across different areas of responsibility. It requires a single point of reference. One clearly identified Project Manager, to whom all day to day decisions can be referred (in whatever democratic manner best suits the particular environment), will mean one centre of responsibility. Shared responsibility usually becomes no responsibility at all.

Where does the Project Manager come from?

Often the Project Manager will be appointed from the customer area. Such a person may have skill or experience that will be useful to the project team. However too much technical interest can generate problems. There may be times when the Project Manager needs to stand back from the detail in order to make business evaluations and decisions. As long as the detailed responsibilities are understood and accepted, the source of the project manager does not matter.

Examples

The Project Managers appropriate for our example projects might be:

- Project 1, Office Move: the senior person in the office to be moved, or maybe a person from the Premises Dept?
- Project 2, Exhibition Stand: someone from Marketing?
- Project 3, New Database: someone from IT?

The last example is interesting because in many larger organisations the Project Manager is often appointed from the end-user community (i.e., the customer community), and not necessarily from IT. This demonstrates a swing away from technical specialists running projects to those with a business view. The selection and appointment of a Project Manager can have a major impact on the overall success of the project (see Strategic Project Factors), and is not something to be undertaken in a casual or offhand manner.

The Role of the Project Manager

The detailed role and responsibilities of the project manager should include:

- to identify project scope, objectives and constraints, and to obtain agreement to them
- to plan the project, at an appropriate level
- to monitor progress against the plan
- to ensure that appropriate quality work is being carried out
- to devise corrective actions for problems
- to inform and advise the Sponsor and the Customer of progress & potential problems

Just like the role of the Project Sponsor, the role of Project Manager cannot be taken lightly. It must be clearly understood and accepted by the proposed manager before the role is formally adopted.

To complicate matters further, it is very common for the Project Manager to be a resource (i.e. member of the team) on the project. Indeed, it may be that the project manager is the ONLY resource available to the project. These situations make it even more important to get the detailed responsibilities sorted out before the project gets fully under way. We may be able to blame someone else later for not realising that they were supposed to do xyz, but it doesn't help the project towards a successful conclusion. Indeed, if a project gets into the blame stage it has probably lost its main chance of success. All that is left is a mess which someone has to sort out.

Other Roles

Some projects may involve other people with supporting roles. Examples might include:

- Auditors (internal or external)
- Health & Safety Inspectors
- Legal Advisers
- Personnel Specialists
- Specialists (e.g. telephone engineers)

These roles play more of a part during the planning of a project and will be dealt with later.

Combining roles

In many small projects it is not necessary to find separate people to play each of the three roles. It is common to combine roles so that, for example, one person may be both the customer and sponsor. As long as the responsibilities of each individual are understood and accepted at the outset (they can always be reviewed later if necessary) and as long as all the likely needs of the project (in terms of authority, decision-making, communication etc) are covered, there is no harm in combining roles.

SPM1, Project Definition

Once the people and the roles have been matched up, it is a good idea to document the arrangement. The form SPM1, project definition, contains space to write the names of the Project Customer, Project Sponsor, and Project Manager. If you want to document the detailed responsibilities, then a separate sheet can be used.

Individual team members

It is not usual to produce detailed responsibilities for every individual member of the project team. However, in some circumstances, it might pay off. When someone is going to undertake a project task outside their normal job, then a short responsibility statement may be of assistance both to the Project Manager and the individual.

For example, on the Office Move project you assign the office junior the job of canvassing views on decorating, colour schemes and coming up with proposals. This task would benefit from a simple note detailing responsibilities, especially in the budget area!

Summary

You must avoid the 'I thought you were going to do that' situation. You can take steps to define clear and accepted responsibilities at the project initiation stage by appointing a project customer, a project sponsor and a project manager.

The details of the individual roles may vary from one project to another. They may need to be reviewed and changed as a project unfolds, but as long as you begin with a defined start position you can cope with all sorts of changes and set-backs.

Chapter 4

Project Planning

Why don't people plan?

Many people get hung up on the definition of a plan, saying that they don't have time to produce one. This probably means that they have the wrong idea about what a plan should look like. They assume that a plan needs to be a complex, graphical document, showing how every minute of every day will be used.

This misconception about the form and content of plans is particularly wrong for small projects. People sometimes say 'If I spend all my time planning then I won't be able to do the work!' How wrong they are.

What is a plan for?

Here are some of the questions that are often asked during a project:

- Can it be done?
- Will it be finished on time?
- When do you need the printers to deliver it?
- The printers will deliver one week late – does this matter?
- I need to take Jenny away for something else. OK?
- How can we be sure that the end product will work?
- Can you also include...?

• The directors are visiting on Friday; what progress can you show them?

• How much will it cost?

None of these questions can be answered with confidence without some sort of plan. Even if some of the 'variables' have already been decided (e.g., you've been told the end date before you start!) there are so many variables to juggle that some sort of written plan, however scribbled, is always better than 'I've got it all in my head'.

More Excuses

While we are on the subject, people put forward many reasons for not planning. Let's examine some of the more common ones:

• **As soon as I write it all down, it all changes**:
Yes, of course it does, but it's not the act of writing it down that causes it to change; things change anyway. The value of having a written plan is that you can analyse and manage the impact of the changes.

• **It takes too long to plan**:
This is only true if you are going about it the wrong way.

• **If I write it all down then I'm stuck with it; people will use it to hit me with if things go wrong**:
How sad! A more positive viewpoint would emphasise the need to gain involvement and commitment from others by using a project plan.

• **I've got it all in my head**:
Maybe, but can you also do 'What if's' in your head? What happens if you are ill?

If a plan has to be able to answer these questions what should it look like? A full blown, big time project plan would actually be a package of related documents, ranging from a full schedule (in the form of a Gantt Chart), through a critical path network, and on to a cost plan or budget. At the other end of the scale a small project may be perfectly well served by a simple task list. Other types of plan might include a wall planner, a diary and so on.

For most small projects a task list is enough, but we will identify ways of making it more useful by, for example, adding target dates, people's names etc.

Gantt Chart

Critical Path Network

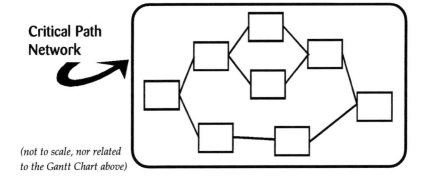

(not to scale, nor related to the Gantt Chart above)

Project Phase/ Task List SPM6

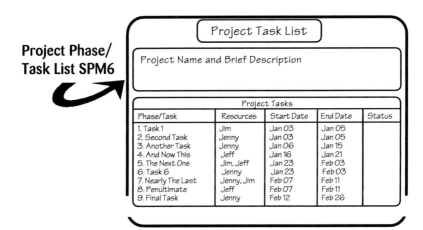

Physically the task list could be hand written, typed, word processed, on flipchart, white board or Lego bricks! Whatever its format, the plan should have the following practical characteristics:

- easy to amend (remember, it will change)
- easy to read (for you and everyone else)
- easy to distribute (if the project team need personal copies)

Finally, depending upon the particular project, the plan may also need the following characteristics:

- ability to show costs/budgets
- ability to show named resources (e.g. People – Jim; Machines – Mobile Crane; Services – company lawyer)

The level of project plan we will focus on for SPM is the task list, with resources, target dates and costs. This is the minimum. There may be enhancements in the areas of risk management, quality management, change management, and multiple project management. These various extensions will be dealt with later.

How do I compile the plan?
Where the plan comes from is an interesting question. It is a great temptation for the project manager to compile the plan 'privately', involving no other members. This may seem like a good idea. The plan emerges quickly, with no interference, but a plan produced this way lacks width of vision.

Who can help you?
While the production of the plan must be a single person's responsibility, input to it must be collected from as wide a range of people as possible. The project manager should ask the following people for views as to what should appear in the plan:

- the project team
- outside suppliers
- the customer
- the sponsor/boss
- technical experts

- legal?
- quality experts
- accountant?
- other project managers

Where else can I go for help?

Various documents can provide sources of useful information at this stage.

- previous project plans
- company standards and guidelines
- quality management system
- technical manuals
- the project brief!

What should go into the plan?

The project manager should cast a wide net when gathering information to put in a project plan. There might even be a team 'brainstorm' to develop a draft plan. This can have the useful by-product of better project team commitment. Don't be afraid of leaving parts of the plan 'to be determined'. Knowing that there are unknowns is better than not knowing at all! It may be necessary to plan in some research tasks, designed to uncover more accurate detail for subsequent planning. Don't forget to include:

- all project work related to the project brief

- planning and replanning time. It's going to happen, so build it into the plan

- progress monitoring and reporting. This is especially required if you need to collect progress information from, say, an outside supplier

- team meetings

- quality reviews. A tricky one here is whether also to allow some 'rework time'; this depends upon your experience with QA in your organisation

- work done by outside resources. Ask the outside suppliers for a copy of their plan and see what sort of reply you get! Seriously, if they produce a plan they will probably produce the goods, and if not, not!

• staff training. Especially training for any members of the project team

• time and tasks needed for the project customer to accept the end product

• all external influences or dependencies should be registered in the plan, as they will be high on the list of potential problems later

How Big is a Task?

The next question and a rather obvious one at this stage, is what should go in the plan? Just two task entries, 'Plan It' and 'Do It', are too high a level, while 200 entries, from 'Sharpen Pencil' to 'Staple Report', are too low level. A balance must be struck in the SPM philosophy — you must not end up with clutter.

The final word on the detail of the plan should rest with the project manager. But here are some guidelines:

• no task should be more than two weeks long (too difficult to control)

• if a task involves a mixture of people, split it into several tasks (too difficult to control)

• if a task produces several different products, split it

• if a task consists of 'activity, wait, activity', split it

• if a task spans a major checkpoint (eg, a main project progress meeting), split it just before the checkpoint

• if a task produces a series of components that each require quality testing, split it

• if a task contains a number of external influences 'or dependencies' split it, and allow some contingency for delays

• if it makes sense to make one person accountable for a part of it, split it

As a very general guideline, tasks of two or three days in length are satisfactory. A 10 minute task may need separate mention if it is vital to the success of the project (eg. a phone call to a supplier for a vital delivery date check). Of course, to do this splitting you must be fairly sure that you know how long each individual task will take. Task estimating is dealt with later.

We can begin to complete the Phases /Tasks List part of SPM1 (or SPM6 if there are more than 10 Tasks) now, so let us see some examples for our sample projects:

Project 1

Project Task List

Project Name and Brief Description **Office Move**

Computers, Contents and People

Project Tasks

Phase/Task	Resource	Start	End	Status
1. Agree Decorations		07/09	15/09	
2. Document Current Network		07/09	15/09	
3. Identify Sales Contingency		07/09	15/09	
4. Decorate Offices		01/10	14/10	
5. Install Wiring		15/10	19/10	
6. Move Furniture		20/10	26/10	
7. Test New Network		27/10	28/10	
8. Move People		29/10	30/10	
9. Complete Sales Move		31/10	31/10	

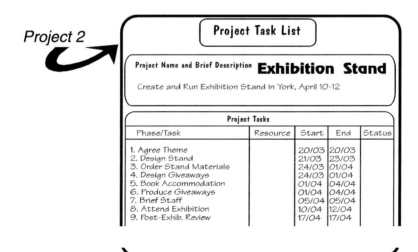

Project 2

Project Task List

Project Name and Brief Description **Exhibition Stand**

Create and Run Exhibition Stand in York, April 10-12

Project Tasks

Phase/Task	Resource	Start	End	Status
1. Agree Theme		20/03	20/03	
2. Design Stand		21/03	23/03	
3. Order Stand Materials		24/03	01/04	
4. Design Giveaways		24/03	01/04	
5. Book Accommodation		01/04	04/04	
6. Produce Giveaways		01/04	04/04	
7. Brief Staff		05/04	05/04	
8. Attend Exhibition		10/04	12/04	
9. Post-Exhib. Review		17/04	17/04	

The importance of sequence

Just jotting the tasks down is fine. It already puts you streets ahead of many so-called project managers, but you ought to consider their sequence. Doing correct things in an incorrect order is a waste of effort. A plan for a larger project might try to express this sequence as a network, with a critical path calculated through the web of tasks. You needn't go that far. A small project will probably have a smaller, simpler task list. Factors that influence sequence include:

- one task producing a component to feed into another task
- chronological, or seasonal, or cyclical, sequence
- simple geographical considerations
- organisational factors (department A must be tackled before department B)
- availability of resources (people, machines etc)
- budget (we cannot afford to do it all at once, so we will do it in several pieces, one after the other)
- availability of external inputs; we just have to wait for something or someone else

Resources (people, machines etc)

You cannot call the task list produced here an adequate plan without allocating resources to the tasks. Even if you think that, for example, you are the sole resource, you will often find that someone else is involved. For example, either the project customer or the project sponsor will be involved, usually at the outset and at the end.

Allocating people to tasks can be fraught with problems. It is no good thinking that it is now 'Fred's problem' just because you've allocated a tricky task to him. Remember who will be first in the firing line if the project fails — you, not him. So the matching of tasks to people must be carried out with care.

Resource Availability

Such information must include:

- does the person have the right skills for the task; if not, what allowance will you make; will you build in training or coaching time (and who will do it, and do THEY have time to do it); will you live with slower progress because of lack of skills or failed quality checks caused by poor skills?

• does the person have the right availability for the task; are they fully available to your project (and what does 'fully' really mean), or are they part time (and how much part time); do you have any history of real availability from this person; will they have to carry out their routine duties alongside the project tasks and who decides on priorities; what about simple things such as holidays and other commitments; have YOU overcommitted them already (motivation through overwork is NOT recognised as a valid motivation strategy nowadays)? *see below for more on this.*

• does the person have the right productivity for the task; do they have appropriate tools etc; how motivated are they towards the project tasks?

Face up to it now

Some of these questions may take you into difficult areas. If you don't try to get answers now, it will be too late when the project starts to run into trouble. It might be that you know who you want, but they are not available. Replanning the project to take reality into account is far better than unrealistic planning based on 'with any luck'. It may be that if you can identify a shortfall of vital skills at the planning stage something can be done about it before the problem hits you.

Where does the time go?

Availability is such a can of worms that it must be tackled as a topic in its own right. People make classic mistakes in this area, such as assuming that someone is available to the project when, in reality, they are also occupied on their routine tasks. Factors to consider in identifying a person's availability for project work include:

A) how many hours per week do they work

B) how many of those hours are spent on parts of their job that must continue alongside the project

C) how many hours per week are spent on administration (timesheets, form filling, progress reports, signing other people's forms, weekly meetings)

The real working week

The maximum number of hours available for project work is A - (B + C). You must then consider which other projects they may be involved in and their relative priorities. It may be that you will be lucky to get seven hours per week out of a key resource. It is better to know this at the beginning (and plan for it) rather than argue about poor performance later on.

Motivation?

Incidentally, there are several standard traps that many managers fall into. They believe that the number of available hours can be increased by isolating the person, cutting them off from all social contact with other people. This is a recipe for disaster. A normal amount of social contact per day is vital to keep people sane. Such managers also rely on overtime and long hours, not realising that many people will work long hours but, because productivity falls off, produce no more than they would have done in a normal working week.

The upshot of all this is that a piece of work that might take person A one full working day to complete might take person B two weeks, simply because of the availability of B. If these factors are understood at the planning stage they can be allowed for.

We can now enter the Resource names against the various tasks on our project plan, as follows:

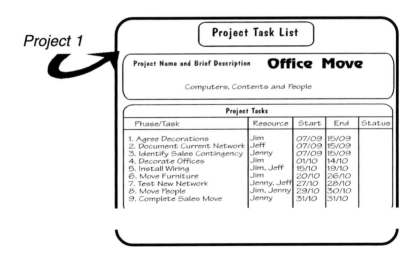

Project 1

Project Task List

Project Name and Brief Description **Office Move**

Computers, Contents and People

Project Tasks

Phase/Task	Resource	Start	End	Status
1. Agree Decorations	Jim	07/09	15/09	
2. Document Current Network	Jeff	07/09	15/09	
3. Identify Sales Contingency	Jenny	07/09	15/09	
4. Decorate Offices	Jim	01/10	14/10	
5. Install Wiring	Jim, Jeff	15/10	19/10	
6. Move Furniture	Jim	20/10	26/10	
7. Test New Network	Jenny, Jeff	27/10	28/10	
8. Move People	Jim, Jenny	29/10	30/10	
9. Complete Sales Move	Jenny	31/10	31/10	

Nearly there?

So, the task list is looking good. It is a list of tasks with resources allocated, and target dates based upon the estimates of the amount of work and the person doing it. Costs can also be entered, as discussed in Chapter 5. You will have thought long and hard about the task list, especially in relation to the people assigned the various tasks. You have documented it all very nicely on SPM1 or SPM6, and the plan meets the various constraints of the project, e.g. end date, budget etc.

Will it work?

Unfortunately, unless you can claim a direct link to a Divine Being, the project will almost certainly not turn out the way it is planned. It is not part of the role description of a project manager to be clairvoyant. Things may happen which are a surprise to the project manager and which jolt the plan. However, there are two things you can do to improve the chances of the project plan being successful. One is the modern and sophisticated technique of Risk Management (considered in Chapter 6). The other is a scrappy and problem-laden technique called Contingency Planning.

One of the big unknowns in any project is 'How long will this take?'. Some estimates are cast iron. If a machine takes one hour to make one widget and we need 20 widgets, we can confidently plan for 20 machine hours, especially if we have a long history of making widgets.

If we have to estimate how long it will take to reconnect the computers to the network once we've moved to the new office, we are on dodgy ground. Even the experts may not commit to a firm estimate.

Contingency allowance

Enter the scrappy and problem-laden technique called contingency planning. This is just about the most abused and misused technique in the project manager's toolkit. Many people approach the subject with dread saying, as they have said to me over the years: 'If I show a contingency allowance in my plan the boss immediately crosses it out'.

The problem in some cases is that we really do need contingency, but it is often the first thing to go when times get tough. I think that part of the reason for this is the way it is added to a project plan. Too many project managers work out their plans with some accuracy, then slap on 10% contingency and hope to get away with it. The whole point about contingency is that you should be able to justify it. A blanket 10% is unjustifiable, so, of course, the boss will cross it off the plan.

A Better way

A better way of incorporating contingency is as follows:

- Look at every single task in the plan. Ask yourself: 'Does this task need contingency?'
- The overwhelming number of tasks will not need any, but, for the few that might, ask yourself two more questions: 'How Much and Why?'

Write down your answers! These answers become essential working papers that support your project plan. If the boss says 'Why do you need all this contingency?' you can explain it, in detail.

We Need the Thought Process

Now for the bad news. The boss may still cross it off the plan. You may think 'Well, what was the point of all that'. Think about it, you identified a dodgy task in your plan, which you are fairly sure will overrun its time allowance. You tried to manage the situation by providing contingency, but that method is not available to you. You must try something else, as the risk has not gone away. For more detail on what else to try see Chapter 6.

The good news is that the boss might appreciate the need for the detailed allowance and accept your plans. I suppose there might be a half way house, where the boss maybe has a different view (or extra knowledge) concerning one of your problem areas. If you have written down your contingency proposals you both have something to discuss!

Summary

You now have a project plan that answers some pertinent questions about the project. You have identified the tasks that need to be executed, their time allowance, their sequence and who will carry them out. You have considered the thorny question of Contingency and have documented the plan in a simple and clear manner.

You could now put the plan in the drawer, and assume that all will unfold just as anticipated. Better still use the plan to increase the chances of a successful outcome. This is the theme of the next chapter.

Chapter 5

Estimating and Budgeting

Time, cost and quality

The job of a Project Manager is simple! After all, there are only three variables in a project, and juggling three things is a relatively simple task.

The three variables are time, cost and quality, and their interrelationship is often illustrated as a triangle:

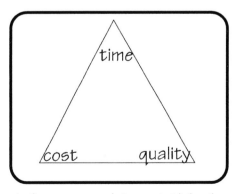

This triangle is dynamic: if you squeeze one factor you stretch the others

Strategic project factors

Earlier we dealt with the Strategic Project Factors. This chapter focuses on using those factors to help estimate time and cost before starting work. Quality is dealt with later.

Hold on, I hear you say, I already know the budget. My boss has told me exactly how much I can spend. He has also told me exactly when I must be finished. So why do I need to spend time on estimating time and cost?

Estimate versus given facts

Lucky you. Two of the most difficult things to establish have been stated right up front; see how easy this project management is! Seriously, just because someone has stated the budget and completion date it doesn't mean that you are off the estimating hook. Questions to ask yourself include:

- is the boss right?
- how did he reach these conclusions?
- when do we need to know he has been mistaken?
- how much leeway do we want if he is wrong?

Answers will vary: Maybe the completion date is immovable. Remember one of the underlying principles of good project management; you must realise that the boss could be right or wrong. Your job is to prove which is which and offer suggestions and alternatives if the boss turns out to be mistaken.

So, even if the cost and time parameters are apparently fixed, you must still go through the estimating process either to reassure yourself that the job can be done within the given time and cost, or to identify possible problems and offer sensible alternatives. Let's begin by estimating time.

Staff hours versus elapsed time

Be sure that you know just what you mean by estimating time as there might be two types of time involved. If you are undertaking a fixed-price job then the number of staff hours involved is crucial; too many and the job loses money. If you are working to a fixed deadline then elapsed time is crucial, because if you miss the deadline you may incur penalties. Many projects have to take both staff hours and elapsed time into account. In this chapter we will look at estimating both these components of 'time'.

Do we need It?

You can simplify the task ahead of you by being clear about the need to estimate staff hours. If you don't need to know them, don't waste time on them. You only need to know staff hours if:

• You need an accurate Staff Cost figure, maybe for arriving at a price for the job

• You are buying in some, if not all, the staff on an hourly basis and you need to know the cost

• You are faced with very tight staff availability and you want to reassure yourself that the job can be handled

• You have a wide range of staff grades involved on the project and you need to track various costs separately

If none of these factors apply on this project you could jump straight to the task of estimating Elapsed Time.

This is an estimate!

You must remember at this stage of the project that you are producing an 'estimate', not a fixed price for the job. Cost (and time) is an estimate or a fact; price is based on a corporate policy decision and need not concern us. However, if the price has been agreed, the estimates for cost (and the cost control mechanisms) become even more important, otherwise the job may lose money.

Let us begin by estimating the staff hours required to carry out the project work. You can see some overlap with Project Planning (Chapter 4) and to some extent the activities of planning and estimating run side by side. However, estimating has its own set of problems and concerns, so it is a topic to be tackled in its own right.

Which units?

Incidentally, I will use the term staff hours but on your project staff days, or even staff weeks, may be appropriate units. The staff hours are the hours of effort required to get a job done. The relationship between staff hours and elapsed time (i.e., how long it takes to do the job) is complex and is dealt with later.

There are two main inputs to this process. Obviously the task list is important, but so is the Underlying Assumptions section from SPM1, Project Definition. There might be assumptions that have a major effect on the project. These must be kept in mind during the estimating process.

Estimating methods

Possible ways of estimating staff hours include:

• Industry standards: guidelines may be available that tell you how many hours are required to accomplish a wide range of tasks, e.g., digging a trench, plastering a wall, writing program code and so on

• Organisation standards: Some organisations will have developed a set of standard times for certain well-defined activities. This makes the estimation of hours a simple arithmetic task

• Similar tasks: For some jobs we may be able to infer likely times from studying other, similar jobs

• Test measurement: Do some work and measure it — sometimes called prototyping

• Ask the 'Worker', who may have personal experience of the job

• Suppliers' manuals: These may give timings for using equipment and so on

• Estimating software packages: Quite common in a number of industries nowadays

• Your own experience: Well, only if you keep reliable records

• Guess: Nothing wrong with this, as a last resort, but back it up with test measurement at the earliest opportunity

Time division?

Don't use simple time division. In other words if you've got six hours to do three things, don't allow two hours for each one. It may be right, but it is usually wrong and painful.

You can note your estimates of staff hours against each task, in the Resource column, on form SPM1 or SPM6, whichever you are using for your phase/task list.

```
┌─────────────────────────────────────────────────────┐
│              ┌───────────────────────┐               │
│              │   Project Task List   │               │
│              └───────────────────────┘               │
│                                                       │
│   Project Name and Brief Description  Office Move     │
│                                                       │
│           Computers, Contents and People             │
│                                                       │
│                    Project Tasks                      │
│  ┌──────────────────────┬─────────┬─────┬────┬──────┐│
│  │ Phase/Task           │ Resource│Start│End │Status││
│  ├──────────────────────┼─────────┼─────┼────┼──────┤│
│  │ 1. Agree Decorations         Jim   12hrs          │
│  │ 2. Document Current Network  Jeff   4 hrs         │
│  │ 3. Identify Sales Contingency Jenny 2 hrs         │
│  │ 4. Decorate Offices          Jim  48 hrs          │
│  │ 5. Install Wiring            Jim   8 hrs          │
│  │ 6. Move Furniture            Jim   8 hrs          │
│  │ 7. Test New Network          Jenny 2 hrs          │
│  │ 8. Move People               Jim   8 hrs          │
│  │ 9. Complete Sales Move       Jenny 8 hrs          │
│  └──────────────────────┴─────────┴─────┴────┴──────┘│
└─────────────────────────────────────────────────────┘
```

Elapsed time

Now consider estimating elapsed time (sometimes referred to as duration, business days or working days). To create a more useful figure, write Start Date and End Date on the Task List on SPM1 or SPM6.

Do we need the detail?

For some tasks the job is very simple. You might be told by a supplier or sub-contractor that a particular task will take two weeks. If you are not interested in the detailed breakdown you can write two weeks against the elapsed time for the task.

Note that this could be made up of 400 Staff hours for 20 people working flat out, or two Staff hours plus a lot of waiting time, but if you are not concerned about the detail, two weeks is good enough.

Fixed length

For some tasks the estimate can be considered as 'fixed'. For example, a trip to Birmingham to check out a supplier will take, say, one working day no matter whether one, two or three people go. Sure, the staff cost will vary, but the elapsed time remains as one day.

More people, less time!

Some tasks respond well to assigning many people. For example, to dig a trench 100m long may take one person 100 hours, or 10 people 10 hours. The staff time will be the same, but the elapsed time will fall.

More people, more time!

Don't get carried away, though, with the idea that throwing more people at a task will shorten its duration. Think of a progress meeting; more people means more time, not less!

The guidelines for estimating staff time can be applied to elapsed time, but bear in mind the temptation (or is it practical necessity?) to round up elapsed time into simple units (eg, five Staff Hours for one person equals one elapsed day). This may be absolutely correct, but the relationship between staff hours and elapsed time is complex, and the elapsed time of every task must be considered carefully on its own merits.

Spurious accuracy

Never lose sight of the problem of 'spurious accuracy'. Who are we kidding if we say that a task will take 3.5 hours? Half a day amounts to the same thing and sounds much more sensible.

The exhibition stand project

Before going on to costs, let's summarise the job of estimating time. It is best seen by looking at the Task List of the Exhibition Stand Project (see opposite).

Start date and end date

The use of Start date and End Date gives us real dates, allowing for weekends, etc, which are much more practical for communication and control purposes.

External costs or all costs?

In producing a budget plan for the project you use form SPM4, Project Budget Plan. This shows, for each relevant item, its cost against the day (or week or month) in which it is incurred.

The use of the term 'relevant item' is deliberate. For many projects it may be necessary only to plan and account for external costs such as goods and services (including human resources) purchased out-

Project Task List

Project Name and Brief Description **Exhibition Stand**

Create and Run Exhibition Stand in York, April 10-12

Project Tasks

Phase/Task	Resource		Start	End	Status
1. Agree Theme	AJ, CKP	(3)	20/03	20/03	
2. Design Stand	CKP	(6)	21/03	23/03	
3. Order Stand Materials	CKP, Supps	(4)	24/03	01/04	
4. Design Giveaways	CKP, PR	(10)	24/03	01/04	
5. Book Accommodation	NL	(5)	01/04	04/04	
6. Produce Giveaways	PR	(15)	01/04	04/04	
7. Brief Staff	AJ, CKP	(4)	05/04	05/04	
8. Attend Exhibition	CKP, Sales		10/04	12/04	
9. Post-Exhib. Review	AJ, CKP	(5)	17/04	17/04	

(all staff times in hours)

side the company. Many organisations are perfectly happy with this type of budget, whereas some go a little further wanting to see the internal staff costs of the project included in the budget.

What are the elements?

Just as in estimating staff hours, you need to ask the question 'exactly what do you need to include in an estimate of staff cost? Elements that must be considered (and maybe excluded from the project costs) include the following:

- staff costs for the project team; or are they a simple company overhead?

- staff costs of any assistance given by the end customer (or is that something for the customer to worry about?); this is especially tricky if the customer is an internal one (same organisation as ourselves)

- purchases (and depreciation?)

The calculation of hourly rates is beyond the scope of this book, as is the apportionment of overheads etc.

Calculating staff cost has already been made easier by carrying out a detailed estimate of staff hours. Once the hourly or daily rates are known, the calculation of cost from hours is simple.

Other factors that contribute to the cost of a project include the following

• People: yes, all the staff hours we've talked about, but also recruitment, training, travelling, accommodation, expenses, subsistence

• Equipment: purchase or rental of equipment needed to undertake the project; maintenance; communications facilities

• Software: purchase or rental; maintenance: training; installation

• Supplies: consumables (paper etc); cabinets, filing, desks; tools

• Additional: office/working accommodation; storage; printing; publicity

In order to complete the project budget you need to be sure when the various costs will fall due. Some will be one-off costs (for example, a purchase of equipment), some may recur during the project (say, travel and subsistence associated with work done at another office), and some may be continuous throughout the project (costs of temporary staff).

Form SPM4 enables you to plan the costs in detail, opposite is an example based upon the Exhibition Stand project.

SPM4 **Budget Plan for Project:**

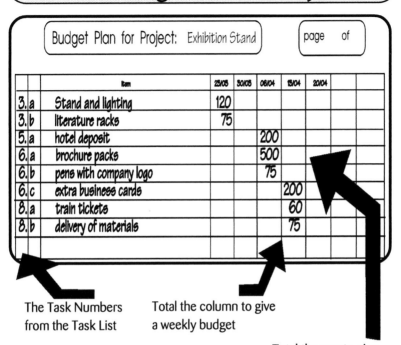

Budget Plan for Project: Exhibition Stand   page   of

		Item	23/03	30/03	06/04	13/04	20/04		
3.	a	Stand and lighting	120						
3.	b	literature racks	75						
5.	a	hotel deposit			200				
6.	a	brochure packs			500				
6.	b	pens with company logo			75				
6.	c	extra business cards				200			
8.	a	train tickets				60			
8.	b	delivery of materials				75			

The Task Numbers from the Task List

Total the column to give a weekly budget

Total the row to give a Task budget

Chapter 6

Managing Risk

A Risk Strategy?

'And now, with any luck...', or, 'How was I to know that they would do that?...', or 'If only I had thought of that earlier.'

Sad, but many people adopt one of those positions at some stage during a project. Obviously, you cannot be clairvoyant. The job of project manager does not include the skills of seeing into the future, but all too often we leave things to luck when, in fact, there is a better way.

Things will still go wrong...

Risk Management is a simple but powerful technique. It is not totally foolproof in that things will still go wrong, but its use can seriously increase the chances of project success.

As with many topics in this guide, we need to start with a few definitions or, at least, a few simple descriptions of what I mean.

Project Risk Assessment

There is a range of Risk Assessment methods which are often used at the start of a project. These methods attempt to identify the risks involved in a project before the project starts and are often used during the feasibility study stage. They aim to highlight factors surrounding the project which militate against project success and prompt the project manager (and sponsor) to change the basis of the project to lessen the risks.

This book is not concerned with such methods. Remember, we took the stance that the decision as to whether or not the project would start had already been made. We are focusing our efforts on making that project a success.

Plan Risk Management

So, I am going to look at a Risk Management technique that takes a project plan as its starting point. It attempts to make that plan more robust, more capable of dealing with the problems that life will throw at the project. The Risk Management exercise is the responsibility of the project manager, but as the outcome of such activity usually puts up the cost of the project, the sponsor must be informed and consulted over intended Risk Management proposals.

During this chapter you will refer to SPM1, Project Definition and SPM2, the Risk Management Form.

The exhibition stand risks

Just to make sure that you understand what I mean by risk, let us look at one of the example projects in a little more detail and jot down a list of some of the things that could go wrong with it. So, for the Exhibition Stand project, let's examine the project plan (Chapter 4) and list the possible problems:

- Stand design does not fit stand
- Stand design not liked by staff
- Stand materials arrive late
- Accommodation unavailable
- Giveaways too expensive
- Giveaways not ready in time
- Key staff not available to attend

Even in a simple project plan you can quickly write down a list of potential problems. If you were to call the project team together to add their views the list would be even longer!

But is it likely?

Of course, some risks are rather remote. I suppose a mathematician could tell me the chances of a jumbo jet crashing onto my office while I am writing this book, but frankly I don't lie awake at night worrying about it.

Also some things may be possible, even likely, but their impact might be small; if my unreliable coffee machine breaks down again I shall be upset, but I shall carry on typing!

These two characteristics, the probability of something happening and its potential impact should it happen, are the two defining characteristics of any risk. It is these two characteristics that you must identify and evaluate in order to manage the risks in your project.

Four stage approach

The technique of risk management has four main elements, as follows:

- identification and assessment
- prevention
- containment
- replanning

The technique is simple but very powerful, and we will look at it by using the example from above, the Exhibition Stand project.

Assessment

Having identified the things that could go wrong, you need to assess them, their probability and their impact. You can use a simple system of assessment. H meaning High, M Medium, and L Low. Some people add K for Killer — there is a place for this, which I will illustrate later. You can evaluate the risks in a simple table: The column headed 'P' gives the rating for Probability, and the column headed 'I' a rating for Impact.

	P	I
• Stand Design does not fit stand	L	H
• Stand Design not liked by staff	M	L
• Stand Materials arrive late	H	H
• Accommodation unavailable	L	H
• Giveaways too expensive	L	M
• Giveaways not ready in time	H	H
• Key staff not available to attend	L	H

Focus

You can now focus on say, High probability/High impact risks. These, by definition, are likely to occur and will cause us problems.

Incidentally, the use of K for Killer is usually coupled with a Low Probability problem that has a Killer effect; such 'L' Probabilities will need very careful consideration.

Risk acceptance

This 'focus' concept is very important. In very few projects can you ever 'manage' all the risks. You might not have the money, time or knowledge to change the situation, so just accept the risk as being present and monitor it closely during the project. You may decide, in these cases, to build up the containment side (see opposite).

I'm not saying that it is safe to ignore the Medium and Low risks. You may need to come back to them later, especially if they are coupled with Killer Impact, but you can begin with risk management of High Probability /High Impact events.

Prevention

The second stage of risk management — prevention, aims to reduce the probability of the risky event happening. Look at each H/H event and try to identify ways in which the probability could be reduced. You can then build those activities (which, in risk terms, are called preventative activities) into the project plan.

For example, for the Exhibition Stand project we could reduce the probability of the stand materials arriving late by using only standard fittings from our suppliers catalogue, by warning the supplier of the tight timescale or by reusing materials left from last year etc.

Note that arranging a second supplier does not prevent the first supplier from late delivery; this is really a containment or contingency activity as you will only use the second supplier if the first one lets you down.

It has a cost

Preventative activities will definitely be carried out, so they probably put up the cost of the project. They need resources and may need to be slotted into a particular place in the plan. The unfortunate thing about them is that, with few exceptions, no matter how many such activities you put into your plan, it will be impossible to bring the probability of a risk down to zero.

Containment, or Contingency

The third stage of risk management will be more familiar to many of you, it is concerned with contingency planning.

Having done your best to prevent the risk from happening, you must now take the rather pessimistic step of assuming that the problem has occurred and ask yourself: 'What would we like to have had in place in order to reduce the impact of the problem?'

The answer to this question may be a series of activities that should be carried out. They are called 'Contingent' or 'Containment' activities.

Examples of containment activities for the 'Stand Materials Arrive Late' risk in the Exhibition Stand project are:

- use last year's stand
- hire a basic stand from organisers
- order from second supplier

Test the contingency plan!

Containment activities are significantly different from preventative activities. The hope is that they are never needed so you shouldn't clutter up the plan with them. However, you may need to test them out, just in case you need them. It would look daft if the much-vaunted contingency plan didn't work! In the Exhibition Stand example it might be time to get last year's stand out of the basement and see what condition it is in before it is pressed into service.

If they don't clutter up the main plan, where do we keep them and what links them back into the main plan? This takes us to the fourth and final stage of risk management: replanning.

Replanning with triggers

Containment activities may lurk on a subsidiary plan. The back of another envelope? But the main plan may need 'trigger activities' built in. These trigger the appropriate containment action as soon as the problem is detected. The name trigger activity may sound very grand, but triggers are usually activities such as progress meetings (especially with a supplier), a quality check or the test run of something. In short, triggers are actions which you were probably going to carry out anyway in order to establish some facts, but now they have this other vital use.

Who should carry out risk management?

The responsibility for compiling a separate Risk Management plan belongs to the project manager. However, it would be a good idea to involve the whole project team in identifying risks and their preventative and containment activities. Very often the author of a plan can be blind to the risks it contains. If there is no project team, try giving your draft project plan to that nit-picking, critical soul found in every organisation. You may get back some useful comments concerning risky elements!

Form SPM1, Project Definition, is the form on which the project manager can establish and agree whether a separate Risk Assessment is required.

SPM1 **Project Definition**

	reqd?		reqd?
Risk Assessment		Project Quality Plan	
Change Management Sheet		Project Budget	

SPM2

If we assume that a Project Risk Assessment is required, then the project manager can apply the four stage approach outlined above, and record the proposed Risk Management activities on SPM2, Project Risk Assessment (see opposite).

There is space on SPM2 for five separate risks. If there are more, simply use more forms — or change the project as it is obviously very risky!

There will be risks for which no prevention can be identified (eg, bad weather); for these you must have plenty of Contingent Activities.

Summary

Remember the old adage; an ounce of prevention is worth a pound of cure. This is a good practical guide for Risk Management. Preventative Actions stop problems occurring, and this must be a worthwhile project management activity.

SPM2 Project Risk Assessment

Risk:

Preventive Actions:

Contingent Actions:

Trigger Actions:

Chapter 7

Controlling the Project

Control strategies

Project managers adopt a variety of strategies when it comes to managing a rolling project:

- look, just get on and do it (*abdication*)

- that last task you just completed was £8 over budget (*obsession with detail*)

- the plans were excellent; what could possibly go wrong? (*blind ignorance; lack of imagination*)

- you'll have to work harder to make up lost time (*desperation*)

- I told them what had to be done; I expect them to do it and heaven help them if they let me down (*persecution*)

Retreat into 'Work'

Statements, similar to those above, are usually made just as the project really starts to go wrong. Even these strategies are better than those of project managers who have no idea of the status of their project and who hide behind project 'technical activity' for instance, instead of carrying out some simple project control.

A small project will not require or justify a draconian, overbearing or bureaucratic form of control. So:

- endless meetings   — are out
- heavy progress reports   — are out
- simple checklists   — are in

Face up to reality

The simple checklist which forms the backbone of SPM project control is based on a simple philosophy; project control should help us to **FACE UP** to reality. Here is the checklist:

F	Facts about progress
A	Assurance about quality
C	Confirmation about costs
E	Early warning of potential problems
U	Update the Plan
P	Publish the Plan

Now consider each of these statements in turn.

Facts about progress

How do you measure progress at the moment? Do you simply ask project team members: 'How is it going?' They reply 'Fine', and you delude yourself by thinking that the project is on track.

They will not necessarily be lying but team members are human beings. They will be:

- optimistic — we think we can get it done in the time

- ignorant — we're not even sure what we have to complete and by when

- members of a go-for-it culture — we want to give it our best shot and not let anybody down

- afraid of the boss

> • unschooled in project management — we feel that we might be running a bit
> late, but we won't bother the project manager with our problems
>
> ... we don't always give or receive facts.

Let me say, though, that I am not obsessed with facts to the exclusion of everything else. The manner in which people tell you things can be as important as the actual progress report.

Non-verbal communication

For instance, if you ask someone 'How is it going?' They say 'Fine', but appear to be about to burst into tears it is clearly not fine! Trembling and non-verbal communication will normally tell you a lot. There is still a place for sensitivity and interpersonal skills, even on a small project.

Back to facts. How can you collect irrefutable facts about progress? Don't attempt it by asking 'How is it going?' You will learn something, but it won't be factual. Do it by asking to see completed deliverables or products. Examples include completed reports, printed publicity material and a completed exhibition stand.

Exercise a little sensitivity over how you ask the questions, but be adamant in your own mind that a completed deliverable means DONE and an incomplete deliverable means NOT DONE.

Sensitivity

The same question can be asked in different ways. There's the demand: You should have finished that, let me see it now. Then there's the request: You should have finished that by now, let me see it? Its all in the intonation, enthusiasm, interest and other positive good vibes that you can get into your voice and manner. Show them that you are interested in what they have produced and they will be proud to show you. Drag it out of them, and they will be reluctant to show you.

Why do I put so much emphasis on completed deliverables?

> • A deliverable can be tested, checked, weighed, measured or whatever; in
> short, its quality against a specification can be proven. Work done on time, on
> budget, but below spec. is a real problem to the project manager, as it probably
> has to be done again. Deliverables are measurable proofs of progress.

- Completed means completed; it is the easiest check of all. The project manager does not want to be told 'It is 80% complete'. This is useless and dangerous information.

- Complete = complete = *no more managing*
  not complete = not complete = *needs more managing*

Confirmation of costs

As each piece of work is completed you can calculate the actual cost. It may have taken much more time than originally planned to arrive at a specific milestone on the project. This will probably mean that the costs are over-running. This must be identified and the implications for future costs established. This is covered in more detail later.

Early warning of potential problems

It is all very well trying to understand where the project is at present. However, project management is also concerned with *acting* on present information to *alter* and *control* future events. What this means is that the project manager must learn to interpret control facts and identify their implications.

Only one week late?

For example, the project manager discovers that one of the key personnel suffered a sporting injury that kept him off work for one week. The sportsman is now back at work, fully recovered.

- Fact: one week lost on particular tasks
- Implication: not great, probably no further loss of staff effort

Further delays to come

But here is another example: the project manager realises that one of the key team members is not as skilled in an important area as was hoped.

- Fact: a particular task took twice as long as planned
- Implication: maybe all future tasks assigned that this person will also take twice as long as planned

These two simple examples show the importance of extending from facts into implications for potential problems. As a project manager you are not expected to be clairvoyant; you are allowed to be surprised by something (eg, Jim Smith can lay carpet tiles at only half the speed of Harry Brown). However, you are expected to learn from your project progress so you are not surprised by the same things twice (Oh look, Jim is still taking twice the time as Harry).

So, the collection of facts about progress must also feed into the early warning of potential problems.

Back to the project definition

Another useful piece of input to this early warning process is the project definition, especially the underlying assumptions section. If the project manager discovers that one of the assumptions is invalid, then this might have a ripple effect down through the project. Remember **FACE UP**; it really is the project manager's responsibility to face up to the reality of the project. Work out the full bad news position (or good news, of course) and take or recommend the appropriate corrective action.

Before talking about the UP part of the control acronym **FACE UP**, there are a few practical details about progress that need to be considered.

Better progress meetings

With a focus on deliverables firmly to the fore, you can see that a progress meeting, for instance, changes from a recital of percentages of progress to a display or 'examination and acceptance' of a range of completed deliverables.

Such a reliance on completed deliverables is absolutely essential when the people doing the work are not under the direct line management control of the project manager. For example, if the work is being carried out by outside contractors, getting hold of facts about progress can only be achieved by the examination of completed deliverables: a decorated office, a tested wiring system, a set of skilled and trained users of a computer system.

Control takes time

There are several implications to this approach. One is that project control takes time (but what is the alternative?). The other is that project control should be linked to events on the plan that produce testable deliverables and not linked to simple events such as the end of the month.

Meetings linked to events

In other words regular weekly or monthly progress meetings may be useless if there are no significant deliverables to examine.

Unfortunately, many bosses, sponsors etc. like to have regular progress reports or meetings because they think that is control. Maybe no-one has explained to them the benefits of another way.

A motivational factor

If it is tackled in a positive and supportive manner, then control via deliverables can be turned into a highly motivating, target-based project planning method. If the project manager can specify in advance what has to be produced and how it will be accepted, the person tasked with producing that product will stand a good chance of organising themselves to be successful.

The other side of this coin is that if the project manager cannot specify these things in advance, how can anyone be expected to do a good job?

Test it

A final point on how to collect facts. Don't be afraid to use old-fashioned techniques such as observation, measurement, tests and trials. For example, if someone is building you a computer system that is required to process 30 customer enquiries per hour, test it, time it and measure it under all appropriate conditions.

Back to our acronym: **FACE UP**. It should be obvious by now that FACE is about the collection of information and understanding what it means, UP (UPdate the plan, publish the plan) is concerned with formulating and taking corrective actions. So, now let's look at UP.

Update the plan

Being realistic about it, the options open to a project manager faced with a replanning job are probably these:

> • **Scrap the Project:**
> The sponsor will need a lot of convincing about this; accurate plans and progress facts will be essential

• Extend the end-date:
If this is the only way out then it must be taken. Often, the project manager might have only one shot at this corrective measure, so the identification of a new target date ought to be accurate and binding. Quite a careful replanning operation may be needed in order to convince the powers that be that more time is needed.

• Draft in more resources: (people, machines etc)
For this option to stand any chance of working, the project manager must know which type of extra resource (and when) would make the required difference. Just throwing more hands at a project that is in trouble will probably make things worse because of increased strain on the project manager.

• Spend More Money:
Someone is bound to ask How Much? Why? When? What For? The project manager must have answers ready in advance.

• Reduce the size of the project:
The project manager could consider leaving out some of the work, either permanently or temporarily (we'll do these things in Phase 2). To make any sense out of this option, the project manager will need to have a clear understanding of the sponsor's and/or end customer's view of the priorities. It will be no good proposing to cut out the vital elements of the project, leaving the customer with a few inconsequential bits and pieces. Negotiation with the customer is vital for this option.

• Reduce The Quality:
Do a poor job! Seriously, although conventional wisdom says one should never reduce quality, it is always worth thinking about. Maybe the original definitions of quality targets, quality products and so on were too optimistic. Perhaps the end customer might accept lower quality in some areas in order to get the end product delivered on time.

To round off this section about Updating the Plan, let me summarise:

• use your plan to confirm that your proposed corrective actions really stand a good chance of solving the problems
• use your plan to gain approval of your proposed corrective actions from the

sponsor. Often the project manager does not have the authority to implement the corrective actions. The usual route is for the project manager to recommend a course of action to the sponsor, who then approves the recommendations.

Publish the plan

Whom do you need to tell that things have changed? Well, anybody affected by the changes. It is easy to overlook the fact that many of the resources involved in your project are probably involved in other projects as well. A slippage on one project might have a knock-on across a range of projects elsewhere.

Having said that the project manager should publish the amended plan as soon as possible, though there may be times when it is not necessary to be quite so quick. If the slippage is not great and if the project manager can get the project back on track before the next major checkpoint, and if there are no changes to resources outside the immediate project team, then maybe the plan can be updated but not published.

Generally speaking, though, on a small project there are no major intermediate checkpoints, just the end-date. The project manager probably has to publish!

In summary, Project Control helps us to **FACE UP** to reality:

F	Facts about progress
A	Assurance about quality
C	Confirmation about costs
E	Early warning of potential problems
U	Update the Plan
P	Publish the Plan

It may be painful, but the alternatives are worse.

Chapter 8

Managing Quality

What is quality?

The basic answer is simple: Quality is what gives complete customer satisfaction, using the word 'customer' in the wider context of 'someone who receives something from us'. This is true for every kind of customer, whether internal or external. Some customer's needs will be sophisticated, others much less so, but all will judge the quality of what they receive by how their needs and expectations are satisfied.

There is no such thing as absolute quality, as it means different things to different people, depending on the circumstances.

Quality matters as much in services as in products, so let us try to define quality point by point. It can be a difficult thing to pin down. We all recognise it when we experience it, but how can it be put it into words?

BSI definition

"Totality of features and characteristics of a product or service that bear on its ability to satisfy a given need." What a mouth full!

A working definition

Basically quality is giving the 'customers' what they want, at the right cost, on time, every time.

In the fast food business, for instance it might be fairly easy to specify the quality criteria for the process of serving customers. Indeed, for most processes that produce an end product or service, quality criteria can be devised fairly easily. But, what does 'quality' mean in the context of project management?

Taking the above definition, piece by piece, you can relate quality to project management.

Elements of Quality

Giving the customer what he or she wants. But who is the 'customer'? The contractual customer of our product or service, or the user of that product or service? It may well be both. Quality means communicating with the customers of the project to ensure that their requirements are understood and agreed at the outset and that the end product will actually do the right job, effectively. Designing the product to meet customer requirements, using faultless procedures for, say, construction, reliable bought-in services/components, skilled personnel, and so on.

At the right cost. Costs are related to quality expectations: a low cost can lead customers to expect a low quality product and a high cost to a high quality product. But they still expect that product to fulfil its specification and function. For example, a cheap paper cup will be expected to hold water just as well as an expensive china teacup. What customers are looking for in a quality product is value for money.

Costs can be related to the project. Most projects have budgets and one of the common problems of managing projects is budget overrun. It is no good giving the customer a high quality, high cost product if it's not what they want and it's going to break the bank and eventually the organisation. A Rolls Royce solution to a mini-car problem may be satisfying technically, but may be in the wrong league when it comes to costs.

On time. Timing is almost always a vital quality element of a service or product and can be another common cause of project problems. The 'perfect' service, set up too late to take advantage of a business opportunity will be a useless white elephant and a source of acrimony and embarrassment.

And more terminology

Two other well-known and poorly understood quality terms must be dealt with before we go much further. A clearer view of 'Quality Control' and 'Quality Assurance' will help you relate quality to project management.

Quality Control

Let us take Quality Control first, as we all tend to know this one better. Quality Control consists of all the checks, inspections, reviews and monitoring activities carried out to ensure that the project is bowling along correctly and that the service or product under construction is conforming to requirements (remember, the right thing, at the right cost, on time). These QC activities can take the shape of testing something to make sure that it works, trying out a set of operator's instructions to see if they are understandable and so on.

Quality Assurance

Quality Assurance addresses the environment within which the project will take place, to make sure that everything is set up to contribute to a successful outcome. Most QA activity takes place before the project gets under way. The environmental factors to be considered are often expressed in six categories: People, Methods, Machines, Materials, Measurements and Environment.

• People
having the right people (skills, availability), carrying out the right jobs (plans)

• Methods
having predefined methods and procedures for carrying out the various tasks

• Machines
ensuring that you have the right machines and tools to carry out tasks effectively

• Materials
having the right materials, bought from quality suppliers, on time at the right price

• Measurements
measurements are needed to ensure a successful outcome

• **Environment**

environmental factors that could influence the success of the project and how they are managed

To put it another way, Quality Control is a reactive method of Quality Management (checking the work after it has been done) and Quality Assurance is proactive (building the right environment before the work starts).

Getting the QC/QA balance right

Too reactive a style of management can lead to high Quality Costs, because the work has been completed before the checks are made. Quality costs are made up of the quality control activities such as inspection, scrap and rework that come straight off the profit of the project.

There is also another hard message about QC, in that the further down the life of a project a problem is detected, the higher the costs of scrap and/or rework.

A well-known example of this effect was given by the Japanese copier company Ricoh, published in the *Times* in July 1993. Ricoh discovered that if a problem in the design of a new copier was not identified right away the cost of correction built up dramatically, as follows:

phase in which design problem found	cost (US$) of correction
design stage	368
production stage	17000
shipment (i.e. at customer's sites)	590000

Such late identification of faults will also cause other problems (rescheduling, resourcing, recosting), all things that the customer may not pay for.

Quality should be 'built in' by effective assurance, not just 'inspected at' by careful control.

QC Activities

Quality Control activities are:

> • controlling the project (measuring cost, people's time etc.)

- testing sub-assemblies or parts of the end product
- reviewing the end product upon completion

All these 'quality' activities are also core project management activities. As you can see, quality has a great deal to do with project management.

QA Activities

So, let us now put Quality into a project context. Quality Assurance activities are:

• project initiation activities
involved in getting the strategic factors out in the open before we start

• roles and responsibilities
clear assignment and acceptance of personal roles and responsibilities

• project estimating and budgeting
the people and money aspects

• project planning
people, money and timescales

• managing the risks
proactively

A Project Quality Plan (PQP)

As part of project initiation activities you must think about a plan for Quality. PQP is a proactive activity that sets up the environment in such a way that a successful outcome is more likely. This is an optional activity. Many small, low risk projects may not need a special quality plan whereas higher risk projects may benefit from one.

The decision on whether or not to create a separate PQP should be made by the sponsor, guided by the project manager. On small projects, for which no separate PQP is necessary, the elements of QA and QC which are still necessary are covered in sufficient detail in the relevant chapters of this book.

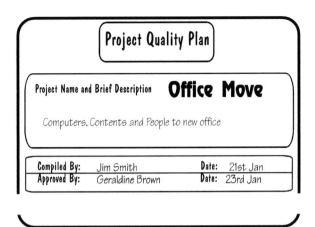

Project Quality Plan

Project Name and Brief Description **Office Move**

Computers, Contents and People to new office

| Compiled By: | Jim Smith | Date: | 21st Jan |
| Approved By: | Geraldine Brown | Date: | 23rd Jan |

SPM5

The rest of this chapter focusses on how to write a PQP for a higher risk project. In documentation terms we will use the standard form SPM5, Project Quality Plan.

How to complete SPM5 Project Quality Plan

The first section is the standard project identification and brief description, and can be completed in accordance with the similar section on SPM1, Project Definition.

Approved by

This PQP should usually be prepared by the project manager and approved by the project sponsor. The signatures of these key people record this fact.

Quality Targets

These targets and criteria must be agreed and signed off at the beginning of the project, so as to avoid 'moving goal posts'. Of course, goalposts might have to move at times, but if you fix their position at the start, you are in a better position to judge the impact of their proposed move later.

The targets now become moments in time when certain predefined aspects of a project will be reviewed against predefined quality criteria, such as delivery date, development cost, quality of product. Delivery date and development cost can easily be specified and measured. 'Quality of Product' can be a rather nebulous phrase, so let us spend a few minutes describing how the quality of any product or service can be expressed. In fact, there are only five quality characteristics of any product or service, namely: *functionality, usability, reliability, performance* and *serviceability*, often referred to by the initials FURPS.

FURPS

FURPS can be best explained by example. Let us take a simple one first. You need to purchase a new washing machine and you realise that there are many models on the market. You can analyse and prioritise your requirements (i.e., your own quality requirements) with FURPS. Here is a set of **FURPS** for a new washing machine:

F   (Functionality)
     well, I don't need any fancy washing programmes, just the standard range

U   (Usability)
     I am experienced at using such machines and do not need a video screen control panel

R   (Reliability)
     top of my list; I need to use the machine every day and it must be reliable

P   (Performance)
     it would be nice if it completed a full cycle within, say, two hours

S   (Serviceability)
     second on my list; if it breaks I want it fixed at once

The most important aspect of FURPS is the agreement that all interested parties must make to the relative rankings of the five characteristics. It's no good having the eventual end user of the product looking for one particular characteristic, say Usability, if the sponsor has decided that Functionality is the main criterion.

The beauty of a quality approach to a project is that discussions and arguments about the relative importance of these characteristics take place before any work or purchasing take place.

And now, **FURPS** for Example Project 3, the Mailing Database Project:

F   Functionality
    yes; we have defined the functions we need, and they must be delivered

U   Usability
    this is a major requirement, as the potential users of this new computer system have very little exposure to this type of system at present

R   Reliability
    being honest about it, this is not a system upon which the daily operation of the company depends; yes, it will be inconvenient if it fails, but we could continue our daily business

P   Performance
    not a big factor

S   Serviceability
    we are concerned that we do not want to install a system which we cannot fix, maintain or enhance easily

You can express FURPS on SPM5 (see opposite above).

This may include assessment against certain standards (product standards such as BSI), methods to be followed during the project, technologies and tools to be used during the project. If a decision is made to deviate from any normal practice then the justification for that decision must be given. For example, you have an ISO9000 Quality System in place and everyone agrees that as you will be building the system in-house you will dispense with the standard company procurement process for the mailing database project. As everyone has agreed to this and it has been documented, you can omit the standard procedure. Again, SPM5 (opposite below).

Implementation strategy
'How will you introduce the end product or service'. There may be no

Project Quality Plan

Project Name & Brief Description

Mailing Database

Name & address system for newsletter mailshot

Compiled By:	Jim Smith	**Date:**	21st Jan
Approved By:	Geraldine Brown	**Date:**	23rd Jan

Quality Targets:
1. Functionality as agreed in memo dated 10th Jan
2. Usability; most important: design for daily operation to be demonstrated before any programming work commences
3. System must be capable of easy alteration in future

Accepted By: Geraldine Brown   **Date:** 23rd Jan

Project Quality Plan

Project Name & Brief Description

Mailing Database

Name & address system for newsletter mailshot

Compiled By:	Jim Smith	**Date:**	21st Jan
Approved By:	Geraldine Brown	**Date:**	23rd Jan

Approach to be used:
1. Standard Company Purchasing selection method not needed, as new equipment will be same as old
2. New Mailing Database must conform to (and be registered with) Data Protection Act
3. New Database must use existing XYZ software, to facilitate easy maintenance

choice. You might have to implement the new service in a 'big bang'. An example from Project 1 (The Office Move) is the way in which the service provided by the Sales Department must not be interrupted during the office move (see below). If this is known and agreed up front then you stand a chance of achieving it; if not, not!

Major Products to be reviewed

This section enables you to decide which products (or parts of the service) will be reviewed and to document in advance how and when we will review them. Once the review has been carried out the findings can be recorded together with the actual review date.

If any corrective action is required to enable the product to pass review, this is agreed and recorded, together with who will carry out the corrective action and by when — the corrective action date. If the product requires a great deal of corrective action, this will incur Quality Costs and may have a detrimental effect on the rest of the project, in timing, costs and resources.

If SPM5 is completed — after consultation between the sponsor, customer and project manager — then the project will start to unfurl in an environment that should lead to a successful outcome.

Project Quality Plan

Project Name and Brief Description **Office Move**

Computers, Contents and People to new office

| **Compiled By:** | Jim Smith | **Date:** | 21st Jan |
| **Approved By:** | Geraldine Brown | **Date:** | 23rd Jan |

Major Products to be Reviewed

Product: Operators Manual   **Target Review Date:** 3rd Feb

Review Method: All 6 Operators + Manager to go through it
(as a 'dry run' of the procedures)

Chapter 9

Managing Change

The two most common reasons for projects going adrift are an unclear or ill-defined definition (scope, objectives, constraints) at the initiation stage and poorly managed changes once the project has started.

If you go through the steps outlined in Project Initiation (Chapter 2), you should reduce the unclear start problems. This chapter focuses on managing project changes.

Change is inevitable

SPM is a practical method. So, once a project definition has been signed, it is not possible to say that the project is frozen for life. It may be a source of constant frustration and aggravation to the project manager to have to change the project, but life is life and any project management approach worth its salt must be able to cope within a changing environment. SPM works on the principle that change is inevitable. What you need is a way of managing those changes and their impact on the project.

I have deliberately kept the approach very simple. There are more sophisticated change management systems available, but these are more appropriate for projects larger than the SPM guidelines.

Types of change

What types of changes are we talking about? Examples might include:

> **• scope:**
> Requests to include new things, drop original items, change the size of some items. For example, in the Office Move project: Can you now also arrange for the old offices to be redecorated after we've moved out.

> **• objectives:**
> A change to the original aim. For example, in the name and address database project, the original objective of designing and building a new system is changed to carrying out a feasibility study and recommending a way forward.

> **• constraints:**
> time (we've got to bring it all forward three weeks); resources (I've got to take Jenny away to work on something more important); budget (we can't spend any more in this financial year, but it is OK for next year)

> **• risk:**
> changes usually entail increased risk, not decreased (we've got to use Dabit & Splashit as decorators, there is no choice).

Three stages

Managing changes to a project is a three stage process:

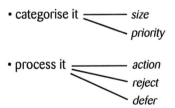

- recognise the change as a change

- categorise it ——— size
                    priority

- process it ——— action
               reject
               defer

Recognising the change

Sometimes a change comes through the door clearly labelled as 'Change'. This might be a statement from the boss, the sponsor, customer, or whoever, that they wish to change the project. Whether it is actually a change or not must be established. It might simply be that the person requesting the change had misunderstood (or never seen) the original Project Definition (SPM1).

Changes that sneak up
The majority of changes sneak up on the project manager, hidden within casual remarks, memos, other people's project progress reports and so on. The project manager must maintain a high level of vigilance in order to detect potential changes to the project.

To do this he or she must have the project definition always in mind, and must carefully check potential changes against the original, signed-off definition.

Baseline
The project definition is the baseline of the project, accepted by all relevant parties and the fixed point back to which all progress will be measured. It is therefore, together with any supplementary documents such as SPM2, Risk Assessment, the essential input to the project manager's change management process.

Once the project manager has detected a change to the project basis, the temptation simply to accept is as a *fait accompli* must be avoided. There is a vital step in the process that must be carried out before any commitment can be made, namely categorisation. Changes should be analysed in two ways: by priority and size.

Priority
essential
the end-product or service that is the subject of the project will be no good without this change (won't work, will be too late, will cost too much etc.)

useful
this change will improve the end-product or service, but it is not essential

cosmetic
exactly what it says

Size
fundamental
this change can only be incorporated by changing the fundamental param-

eters of the project, for example the agreed end date may have to shift, the budget will increase by £xx

tolerable
the change can be incorporated within the current project parameters, maybe by consuming the project manager's contingency, or by cutting back or cutting out something else

trivial
the change is of such limited impact that no significant replanning is required

You may ask why it is worth bothering to analyse and document trivial and cosmetic changes? Well, there are two answers to that question.

Trivial?
Firstly, how does the project manager know that a change is trivial, without stopping to think about it. Often such changes are announced with a degree of ballyhoo that belies their impact on the project; they may be very important in the eyes of their proposer.

A thousand cuts
Secondly, two dozen trivial changes, poorly managed, can damage a project almost to the point of failure.

Limits of authority
So, having analysed and categorised the potential change, we can represent the various combinations in a table which illustrates another aspect of Change Management, namely Limits of Authority.

There are three levels of change to consider. The project manager's 'Limits of Authority' may be spelt out in the Roles and Responsibilities section of the Project Definition. Often it isn't spelt out, but is left to the judgment of the individual project manager.

Some guidelines
As a suggestion for steering the project manager into safer waters, a common approach to 'Limits of Authority' is to agree guidelines such as these:

• essential/fundamental, essential/tolerable, essential/trivial changes must be incorporated, unless the Project Sponsor expressly rules against one

• useful/fundamental, useful/tolerable, must be debated before action, rejection or deferment

• cosmetic/fundamental, cosmetic/tolerable, cosmetic/trivial, and useful/trivial can all be rejected unless the Sponsor expressly selects one for action

priority \ size	fund'tal	tolerable	trivial
essential			
useful			
cosmetic			

Possible Abuse

Now, you may have spotted the flaw in this little system of rules, the categorisation into priorities is open to abuse. The sizing of a change should not be an issue. The project manager, using the project definition and project plans, should be able to justify any estimates of size. However the establishment of priority should be the responsibility of the customer or sponsor. Herein lies the potential for abuse. How often have you seen 'top priority' attached to all changes making them meaningless?

Sign-Off

A meeting to discuss and agree the priorities of changes — and agree potential changes to the schedule — will help in this 'top priority' situation.

SPM has a tool to counteract this potential for abuse. Every proposed change must be signed off before it is actioned. This step may go some way to damping down an over-enthusiastic proposer of changes.

Document the decision
The final step in Change Management is that of Process, which has three possible outcomes:

- **Action:** the change is accepted, signed off and will be incorporated

- **Reject:** change refused

- **Defer:** accepted, but not to be actioned at present. The change may be incorporated in a later project, or in a later stage of this project.

SPM 3
SPM does not impose any form of documentation of Rejected or Deferred changes, but suggests that changes that are accepted for Action should be documented. SPM3 is offered as a way of doing it.

Example
Using the example of the Office Move project, the suggested change of 'Redecorate the old office after the move' can be added to SPM3.

The Office Move Project
The form will be kept with the other project documents (eg, project definition) as it alters or qualifies some of the entries on the original Project Definition. As it is used throughout the project it will provide a history of changes.

In summary, change is inevitable even in a small project. SPM hits the balance of low-overhead practical control together with security and documented agreement.

Change Management

Project Name and Brief Description **Office Move**

Computers, Contents and People to new office

Compiled By: Jim Smith   **Date:** 21st Jan

Change: Redecorate Old Office after all staff and equipment have been moved out

Implications: Not a lot; need to agree decorating scheme with Dabit & Splashit before the move, then let them get on with it

Accepted By: Geraldine Brown   **Date:** 27th Feb

Chapter 10

Reviewing the Project

Are we doing this right?

There comes a time on every project when someone says 'Are we going about *this* the *right way?*' You need to be absolutely clear about what I mean by this question. I don't mean 'Are we on track?' — a simple and valid project control question. I do mean 'Are we doing the right things from a project management point of view?'

The manner in which this question is answered can often have a major bearing on the future direction and success of the project. So you must spend a little time considering the question and a way of answering it that helps in making sensible and positive decisions about the project.

Let us take the initial question apart and focus on each component in turn:

- **someone says:** who is 'someone'
- **a time on the project:** when could or should the question be asked?
- **this:** is 'this' still valid (i.e. has the project changed out of recognition)
- **right way:** what is the right way? Who can ask this question?

Who cares?

Obviously the project sponsor has rights in this area. Why should the sponsor pour good money after bad if the project is so badly run that the money will be wasted?

The project manager ought to be able to ask the question, even if it is asked privately. The project team ought to be able to ask the question, so that they feel that their efforts are being directed wisely. The project customer ought to be able to ask the question, to be reassured that the end product will be all that is required.

With so many people capable of asking the question, there must be a standard approach to this situation otherwise the project manager, who probably will have to provide the answer, will be swamped with a range and variety of time-wasting questions.

Now, let us consider the timing. When would someone ask the question 'are we. . ?'

When is a good time to do this?

There are several times in the life of a project when the question should be asked:

- One of the most obvious occasions occurs when the project hits a large stopping point, maybe when something serious has gone wrong.

- Change the tense of the question and a constructive point at which to ask it comes after the project has been completed. This is the opportunity to learn how to improve and do it better next time.

- A subtle, but valuable, time to ask it happens when a new project manager has to take over, maybe because the previous project manager has been moved on to something else. The new manager needs to take stock of the situation very quickly, as people may be looking for fast action to sort something out.

- A good time to ask the question comes when it is realised that the original project scope, objectives or constraints have changed out of all recognition. A review of them is essential.

Lastly, we need to know what the 'right way' is in order to ask 'are we...' If you can define the 'right way' in a neutral and constructive manner you stand a better chance of reviewing the project against it and winning approval from all parties to any changes.

Who is to blame?

In defining the 'right way' to manage a project and therefore a means of reviewing any project against the 'right way', there must be a method of defining it that satisfies certain criteria:

- Non-personal: For any review to succeed the project players must feel that the project is being reviewed, rather than them as people; roughly translated, this means that a project review must not turn into a witch-hunt or a search for someone to blame

- Checklist approach: So that all aspects are considered

- Quick and simple to operate: To encourage frequent use of the checklist; so that, if necessary, the project manager can carry out a review without stopping the whole project in its tracks or interviewing the entire project team one at a time.

So the SPM project review method consists of a checklist that can be followed in a non-personal manner, producing a constructive review of the key elements of the project, that will either satisfy the concerned parties or bring about a series of positive changes to get the project back on track.

The outcome from such a review is either a formal report to the project sponsor or customer or the Boss, or an informal report for the internal use of the project manager and the project team. Either way, the findings should be documented in some way so that they can be acted upon and not lost in the welter of project paperwork.

A formal 'Project Review Report' may sound rather imposing for a small project, yet it can be a very useful document. If you want to improve your performance as a project manager, you must carry out some project management work, measure what you do and then plan to improve it. A project review report, however informal, can help us become better project managers.

So, here is the checklist. The report should be structured around this list, with a series of recommendations as the final statement:

Basis

- was the purpose of the project clearly defined at the outset?

- did everyone agree?
- did it change as time passed by?
- did the project have a business objective?
- was the end product clearly defined early on?
- were success criteria defined?

Plans

- were there any plans?
- was there a Project Definition (SPM1)?
- were the plans used or just forgotten?
- were they realistic?
- were deadlines, budgets, product targets met?

Personnel

- were the right people available to work on the project, at times and quantities required?
- was the team composed of the right skills and experience?
- was the team productivity acceptable?
- did the team members achieve job satisfaction on this project?
- did the project enhance the team members reputation, skills, development?
- did the team members behave professionally?

Working methods

- were appropriate and useful techniques, standards etc. used?
- how useful were they?
- were appropriate tools used?
- were the facilities acceptable (accommodation, computer facilities etc.)?
- was the level of support satisfactory (training, guidance, clerical etc)?

Project management

- was there any project management carried out?
- was the project manager sufficiently experienced, skilled, trained, supported?
- did the project manager have or make enough time to carry out the project management duties?
- did the project manager have enough authority?

Control structure

- were appropriate levels of control exercised?
- were procedures for measuring progress etc. devised and implemented?
- was the control overhead justified?
- did the project control activities support the team?

End product

- do the customers use it?
- did it fulfil its business objectives?
- will it be reliable, flexible, maintainable, as required?
- will it be cost effective?

So what?

For every one of the questions above, there is the subsidiary question 'So What?' It might be that there were problems with obtaining key people at the required time. Did it really make any difference to the project? If the answer is 'No', then you can merely document your findings; a recommendation for improvement may not be required.

If the answer is 'Yes', then you must devise some recommendations to improve the project management situation for next time.

What improvements can we make?

Recommendations for improvements may tackle the root cause of the problems, or simply point out that certain elements exist in the project management environment and must be endured or accepted.

For example, if a major problem is identified with the time taken by senior management to accept and sign-off the initial Project Definition, either learn to live with the situation — by changing people's expectations about how quickly projects can start — or recommend a change — such that the review and acceptance of Project Definitions becomes a regular feature in the weekly management meeting.

The SPM improvement cycle

The whole reason for conducting a project review is to improve the way in which projects are managed, either the current project or all future projects. Improvement only happens through management action; management action only happens through the presentation of reasoned argument, backed up by facts and recommendations.

The SPM approach to Project Review provides all these elements, and supports a simple self-improvement cycle.

Chapter 11

Managing Several Projects

Just one project?

So far this book has taken you through the main elements of managing a small project, ie, one small project. The overwhelming majority of readers will find themselves in the position of managing several (or many) projects at the same time. In fact, the common mix of responsibilities that form the workload of a typical project manager looks like this:

• a number of packages of work clearly labelled as 'projects'

• a large number of bits and pieces of work, not clearly labelled as anything

• staff management work; recruitment, appraisals (both conducting and receiving), training planning, training delivery, informal coaching, counselling, discipline, writing procedures rules and guidelines

• reviewing other people's work, either formally (in a Quality Review) or informally (just have a quick look at this will you, before I send it out)

• company business; weekly/monthly management meetings, annual meetings, roadshows, open days

• company/social business; sports and social events, work experience schemes

• social intercourse; just talking to people, getting coffee, going to the loo, fixing up a tennis match

• company admin.; filling in timesheets, progress reports, expenses, holiday requests, purchase orders

• the routine job; the project manager's 'own job', whether it is sales manager, accounts clerk, warehouse manager, computer technician; this job, of course, must be fulfilled without noticeable adverse impact

Macho motivation

While we are on the subject of the balancing of demands of a routine (fulltime?) job against the pressures of managing a project, let me state something with which many senior managers may disagree...

It is not motivating to pile a so-called career opportunity on top of a regular job. Macho motivation, by applying multiple pressures to key staff members, is totally discredited as a motivational strategy. Yes, such pressure can get people moving, often through fear, but when the pressure is relaxed the people slow down. Movement caused by external pressure is not the same as, and not as effective as, motivation caused by internal drive.

The effective manager will find out what things motivate every one of the individuals who make up the team and provide those things; this is the only true way to motivate a team of individuals.

This is beginning to sound like a sermon and people management issues are beyond the scope of SPM. However, the common effect of over-optimistic dumping of work (we cannot call it delegation, as that implies thoughtful management) is, among other things, a major cause of project failure and this is a legitimate concern of SPM.

Returning to the analysis of the workload of a typical project manager, you can see that project work may take a very low priority at times. The interesting question to contemplate, and one posed in a different way in Chapter 4, Project Planning is:

'How much time will the project manager be
able to devote to "Project Management"?'

How much time can YOU spare?

People approach this question in a variety of ways:

- **ignore it** – take on too many commitments; wonder why they never get anything done

- **answer it too optimistically** – results as above

- **try to measure it** – the 'scientific' approach with, usually, frightening results

Do you really know where your time goes?

Before taking on the challenge of managing a project alongside your normal work a revealing first step is to measure where you spend your time. Try completing a timesheet for a few weeks. Summarise the results and discuss your findings with your boss. In any event, what you are trying to establish is where your time goes and therefore which jobs you might have to stop, or pass on to someone else, in order to take on some project management responsibilities.

Now, let us assume that you have measured and managed your time. The next question is 'How can you plan and control a multitude of jobs'?

Get the basics down first

Follow this sequence:

- write down all the fixed activities that you must carry out (eg, monthly management meeting, progress report, etc.)

- write down all the personnel management activities you must carry out, that you cannot delegate (eg, appraisal of immediate subordinates)

- write down all your project activities

Diary dates

One effective way of coordinating a whole bunch of small projects is to extract from each project definition the key project dates — when a task must be completed, when a quality review takes place, when a risk trigger must be tested — and write them all into a diary.

Then, at a glance, you can see all the project events due on a certain day. If you have already entered the fixed and unavoidable commitments into the diary, you will be able to identify commitment clashes (either for you or key staff members), knock-on effects of one project delay across other projects, and so on.

Using a Filofax

So, above is an example using a Filofax-style personal organiser as the 'consolidation' mechanism. There are three projects on the go this week, together with some line management tasks.

Wednesday and Friday look particularly busy and could cause problems. The project manager should consider taking action as follows:

- delegate one of the two events on Wednesday, or reschedule if delegation is not an option

- delegate either Colour Scheme job or Recruitment Interview job

- deferring the staff appraisals should be resisted, as the staff concerned might not like to be lower in priority than Agreeing a Colour Scheme!

1	2	3	4	5		
8	9	10	11	12		
15	16	17	18	19		
22	23	24	25	26		
29	30	31				

Using a wall planner

Another simple but effective way of consolidating a number of projects into one clear picture is to use a wall planner. Many people copy the wall planner onto paper (A3 is a good size), which is usually more portable.

The same principles apply as before:

> • write down all the fixed entries first (holidays, monthly management meetings, progress reports, training etc)

> • write down all the personnel management activities next (appraisals, recruitment, induction, training)

> • now write down significant dates and events selected from your portfolio of individual project definitions

Problems of resource clashes, overloading of the project manager and so on should now begin to emerge.

Challenge the priorities

Does it all fit into your time allowance (can you do your week's work within one week?)

If the answer is Yes, excellent!

If the answer is No, then you must challenge and reaffirm the relative priorities of project versus other work. With your plan, even if it is only a simple list of commitments, you have something to take to the boss.

Monitor against your assumptions

Assuming that any problems are resolved, you now have a very important thing to do. You must monitor how your time is actually consumed (yes, even if it means the dreaded timesheet again). Having taken all this trouble to base your future workload on some factual breakdown, it is vital that you verify the actual time consumption. Then, if the actual time spent on certain types of work differs from the intended split you can react quickly and take steps to adjust the balance of your time.

Use a computer?

The planning and managing of a multiple project environment can be made easier by using a computer system (see Chapter 13). However, the computer system will probably only point out clashes; it will not help very much with the initial planning.

Summary

SPM is a method for managing a small project. However, its underlying principles are completely valid in the multiple project environment within which most of us work.

Chapter 12

Managing a Crisis

After all this, a crisis?

Is this where you ask for your money back, or realise that this book really is a practical approach to managing projects?

Yes, of course there will be crises, despite your careful following of all the guidelines encapsulated within SPM. No project management method can overcome all the unknowns; no author can write a series of guidelines in such a way that any reader can be guaranteed perfect success every time.

So, I've got the cop-out in at last!

Make it worse; make it better

We all know that in a crisis there are things we can do that make it worse. Well there are things we can do to make it better, things that help us get the crisis back under control.

I suppose that this chapter is a condensed version of the whole book. In a crisis there are a few basic but vital factors that you must manage. The difficulty is recognising them in amongst the smoke and the yelling that accompanies most crises.

Vital few from trivial many

The theme of SPM is sorting the Vital Few things to do from the Trivial

Many. So here goes for a crisis.

Do you really have crises?

First of all just what is a crisis? If you attempt a definition by listing the attributes of a crisis, a strategy for their management should emerge. Such attributes are usually stated as:

- something unplanned or unforeseen
- very tight timescales, usually forced on us
- changes to resources
- changes to objectives or scope (what we were aiming at, or the size of the job)

Those macho types among us will claim, or even boast, that they live in crisis mode all the time. Well, I wonder about that. If it is true then maybe our personal prioritisation rules need to be examined. Just being busy — even rushed off our feet — does not signify crisis.

I am talking about organisation-threatening events that spring upon you (substitute life, job or whatever is important to you).

The concept of dealing with factors forced upon us within a tight timescale is a common working definition of a crisis.

So what are the vital few elements that must be managed at all costs:

- objectives and constraints
- plans
- roles and responsibilities
- communication
- and, unusually for this book, a few words about behaviour!

Behaviour

Let us start with behaviour. How you act can have a major impact in a crisis, as there is so little time to recover from mistakes. Some don'ts:

- Don't panic, or rather don't panic visibly. Panic is contagious; if people see you panicking then they will panic as well. You can be in turmoil inside, but don't let it show. Calm control is just as contagious; I know which one I'd rather catch. Don't attempt to dispel thoughts of panic by lounging about, though; it is a matter of balance.

• Don't rush into a course of action you will regret later (this often creates several more crises out of the original one). We will look later at what to do to find out facts, but jumping to conclusions without any research is very dangerous.

• Don't be afraid to ask for help; although some people revel in hearing about your problems most people are willing to help. There might just be somebody who has been through this exact crisis before. Bottling things up can be very dangerous.

The crisis checklist

And now, a basic checklist. Analyse the situation as coolly as possible. Establish the following:

- what is actually happening, as opposed to what is being shouted about?
- why it is happening (develop a theory; get facts; test theory; try again)?
- how quickly you have to act before things get seriously worse; especially look for timescales on stopping it spreading or containment activities?
- what might happen if you do nothing?
- who else is involved?
- who else might get dragged in?
- what resources you have available?

This list may seem long, even too much to waste time on. The clever answer to that is 'How much time do you think you have to waste?' Without going through this checklist you will be fighting in the dark.

In reality you may find that the checklist takes all too short a time; you might wish you had more questions to ask.

Now, having asked the questions, tackle the information in this way:

Draw up a preliminary action plan, based around three levels of priority:

• **interim measures:** what has to be done to stop it getting worse

• **adaptive measures:** what could be done to help us carry on 'normal' business in the new circumstances

• **corrective measures:** what has to be done to fix the underlying problem that caused the crisis

Keep your mind clearly focused on the relative priorities. Don't start a philosophical discussion on pollution-free, non-combustible building materials (corrective measures) while the building is still on fire (try some interim measures, ie, put the fire out).

Rules for a simple plan

Some people enjoy a philosophical discussion at any time, even in a burning building, especially if it is your problem to sort out rather than theirs. You must establish a public mechanism for directing and controlling everyone's efforts. This will be a plan of some sort, but there are three golden rules for a crisis plan:

> • keep it simple (otherwise nobody will understand it, and you won't keep it up to date)
> • keep it public (so that you can remind the drifters to get back to the point in question)
> • update it with new info. (because it must change as you move through the crisis)

Real roles work

Review roles and responsibilities, especially from the viewpoint 'Do we really need all these people involved?' If someone has a clear and genuine role they will fulfil it splendidly; if they don't, they will be in the way.

Check your own levels of authority; do you really have the authority to turn off the main power to the office block?

When the 'phone starts to ring'

Open simple lines of communication. As soon as people find out that you are dealing with the crisis your phone will not stop ringing with their enquiries, help, offers of assistance, requests for progress reports, a suggestion that you speak to the press and so on. It is inevitable, but, if you are trying to play a real part in solving the crisis, you will find the interruptions highly damaging.

So, set up a communications centre — someone to answer the phones. Let everyone know that this has been done. Make sure that the project or crisis team keep the communications centre up to date with the situation. In this way the communications person will be able to field a large proportion of incoming calls, freeing you and the team to get on with the work.

Make plans for handling your own normal work and that of the crisis team members. You don't want to create a new crisis out of this one.

Stand back at least once a day and review how things are going against the 'plan'.

Monitor your actions

As soon as you take action monitor its effects. Set up a monitoring mechanism that will last until the crisis is over.

None of this will guarantee that you will manage your way through all the crises that come your way, but if you do tackle them in an orderly manner, people will see that you are trying.

Chapter 13

Using a Computer
Don't do it!

Seriously, why would you want to use a computer to help you manage a small project? As this is a serious question, let me offer some serious answers:

• Firstly, you have a project which is unclear at the start and you want to list a few tasks to get you going, knowing full well that as soon as you start lots of other tasks will come creeping out of the woodwork. You reason that, if the plan is stored on a computer, you can easily add the new tasks when they appear.

• Secondly, you have a project which requires a publishable plan, either to the Sponsor or maybe to an outside Customer, and you feel that a plan printed by a computer might look better than a handwritten list.

• Thirdly, you have heard a lot about the new project management software that's on the market and you want to get something to help you as much as possible; after all there must be something in it.

• Fourthly, you fancy playing with a computer package that will produce lovely looking plans etc.

• Lastly, the boss says 'use this piece of software to manage your project', so you have to at least give it a try.

Am I getting close?

No adverts!

This chapter is aimed at dispelling the myths about project planning systems, setting some guidelines for what to look for if you have to choose one and describing how to use one: a generic one, not a specific one — I'm not advertising anybody's software for them.

I am a fan

If this chapter begins to sound like a diatribe against planning packages then let me declare right away that I'm not against them. I think that they can be of great assistance to a project manager. What really does worry me, though, is the way that many bosses think that once they have allowed you to purchase some planning software you can produce effective project plans.

Tools do not equal skills

If you were to give me a set of chisels it wouldn't make me into a carpenter; just a person with a set of chisels. If the chisels are sharp then I become a dangerous person. Training in how to use chisels does not make me into a carpenter; just into a skilled chiseller.

Giving a novice project manager a piece of project planning software does not make that project manager into a skilled planner, just a person with a piece of software. Training in the software merely makes the person proficient in the software, not a skilled project planner.

GIGO

Unfortunately, the software will produce some seductively well presented documents that look like project plans, but do you remember the old saying 'GIGO' meaning 'Garbage In, Garbage Out'? Well, when applied to plans it means 'Garbage In, Gospel Out'. If you don't know what a project plan should contain and how it should be constructed, the use of a piece of software will be dangerous; you will produce something that looks so good people will believe it.

It can help a little

When making decisions about planning the steps in a project (Chapter 4) a computer cannot help much with:

Planning Decisions
- compiling a list of tasks
- getting them into a sensible sequence
- breaking them into practical units
- estimating size and cost
- identifying resources required
- assigning resources to tasks
- allow for contingency

Planning tools, or management tools

While we are on the subject of putting a planning tool into context, many of them are sold as Project Management Packages. Don't be misled by this, people manage projects not computers. Here is a list of the topics that a project manager should consider when managing a project. Again, a computer is not a lot of help with:

Management Decisions
- Initiation
- Strategic project factors
- Shaping the project into phases
- Project definition
- Roles & responsibilities
- Estimating
- Budgeting
- Managing risk
- Controlling the project
- Measuring progress
- Interpreting progress information
- Replanning the project
- Planning for quality
- Measuring quality
- Managing change
- Reviewing the project
- Managing several projects at once
- Managing a crisis

Where it can help

Now, let us focus on what a piece of planning software can do. In manipulating the plan it can:

- hold the list of tasks, so that you can update it
- hold a list of resources, ditto
- hold target dates, and remind you when events linked to dates are due
- draw and redraw bar charts or Gantt Charts easily
- make many copies of complex lists and charts
- extract tasks applicable to particular individuals, to provide each team member with their own plan
- provide version control of plans, so that confusion over versions can be minimised
- warn you of a resource overload, so that a key person is not accidentally over-assigned
- allow you to produce timesheets or worksheets for individuals
- capture actual time spent (and therefore the actual cost incurred)
- allow you to merge several separate plans together, and identify resource usage across them, so that potential resource problems can be spotted before they occur
- recalculate costs and timescales for work not completed
- print project plans at a summary level, to help senior management to operate without being swamped by the tiny details
- record the thought processes and working details against each task, so that we don't forget why something was done in a particular way

and so on.

Actually, the list is quite impressive so far. There are many more things that can be done, varying from package to package.

But you must know what you are doing

So, I hope that I sound a bit more positive now. I really do think that they can be very useful, but only after the user, be it project manager, specialist project planner, or whoever, has been shown capable of producing effective project plans 'by hand'. By this I mean that the users of such software must know exactly what they require and how they can do it, before they attempt to get a computer system to help them.

One last analogy and then I will become positive and stay positive.

You wouldn't buy an accounts package, give it to a novice accounts person and then rely on them to produce company accounts for the next month end, would you!

If you turn back to my earlier list of planning steps, you can begin to see how you can use a computer to really help:

• **Compile a list of tasks**
not the creative bit, but software can help in several ways:
template plans
• recording what you did last time, so if your current project is similar you may be able to give yourself a flying start by amending a previous plan
• reminding you of the standard tasks you must include (at least, consider for inclusion) if your project must follow a standard pattern

• **Get them into a sensible sequence**
to extend the theme from above, your 'starter' plan (sometimes called a template plan) could also include likely sequences

• **Break them into practical units**
ditto

• **Estimate their size/cost**
ditto estimates

• **Identify resources required**
ditto resources

• **Assign resources to tasks**
It may be possible to build a library of resources (people, machines etc.) that you can call up in every project plan. You don't have to use them all the time, but once you have the library you can incorporate it into whichever plans you desire. It may also be advantageous to record against each resource narrative their capability (but watch out for Data Protection Act implications). Individual cost rates can be held, to help with automatic project cost calculations. The ability to record and reuse individual availabilities is very valuable.

• **Allow for contingency**
There's not a lot that a planning tool can do here, except help to store details of what actually happened last time.

Now, take a look at some of the types of software that might be of use.

You must take a realistic view of the type and level of planning you will actually carry out.

Word processor

Don't spend time and money installing a powerful planning package if you will probably only want to create and maintain a list of tasks, together with their associated target dates and resources. A word processing system will almost certainly be sufficient for this type of planning; simple to learn, simple to use, fit for purpose.

If you want to progress to any of the following:

- bar chart
- weekly resource usage and costs
- merging of several detailed plans into one consolidated plan
- critical path analysis and Gantt Charts

then you should consider these factors before you fire up your sophisticated planning software:

- **Something fancier** – does the size of the project really justify this level of planning?

less than 4 weeks	– almost certainly not
4-8 weeks	– possibly not
more than 8 weeks	– probably

- **Practical considerations** – do you have the computer system to do it effectively?

  Not just performance, but accessibility and portability (if you will be doing most of your work on several different sites, where do you want the plan to be?)

- **Learning on a live project?** – do you really have the skills?

  Will you spend a disproportionate amount of time learning and struggling, only to make a subtle yet dangerous mistake?

If, after considering all the pros and cons, you decide to go ahead, here are a few simple tips to ease the process:

• Conventions

establish, and stick to, a common naming convention for your resources; to a software package JS, J S, Jim and Jim Smith are four different resources and each will be allocated to the maximum; poor old Jim Smith!

• Hours per Week?

be realistic with people's likely availability for project work (most people would find it difficult to give you more than three days per week, or four to five hours per day).

• Holidays

make sure you build in fixed events first; public holidays, personal holidays, company events.

• Blocks

group your tasks into meaningful blocks; this could be very useful when you come to print out the plan, as you could choose to print only at the 'summary' level, in order to see an uncluttered view of the project.

• Printer

use the printer often; it can be very easy to lose sight of the project if your view is limited to a small window somewhere in the middle of a screen.

• Notes

use the built-in note facility if there is one; record as many of your thought processes as you can; do whatever you can while you are building the plan to avoid the 'Now why did I do that' problem three weeks later.

I'm sure that there are many more hints and tips; read the manual that comes with the software for tips that are specific to the package you intend to use.

Now go for it

Let me repeat something I said earlier; I am a fan of PC-based planning tools, but only because I know how to produce a project plan. Don't think that the tool, however sophisticated, will let you off the problems of project management. Don't expect too much, but they can be of valuable assistance.

Chapter 14

Implementing SPM

Are you really going to do It?

So, you've read the book; do you really want to implement SPM? You must ask yourself why? Which aspects of your current operation are you hoping to improve?

It is very important that you are clear about this. Without such targets you could just fritter away your efforts in a haphazard fashion. In fact, you should view the implementation of SPM as a project in its own right and a project needs:

- objectives
- a plan
- roles and responsibilities
- resources

Treat it as a project

At the end of this chapter you will find a typical project definition for implementing SPM. Remember, it is only a typical example and would need tuning to meet your own circumstances. We will now look at how to tune the example plan.

SPM begins with Strategic Project Factors. Here are a few questions for you to consider:

• Who will be responsible?
who will be involved in this implementation project; who will manage it; who else might be involved in drawing up specific guidelines or standards?

• Who will be involved?
who will use SPM; how much training will they need (training in SPM or training in project management as well)?

• By when?
what is the time scale for implementing SPM? In phases, or in a big bang approach?

• Any risks?
anyone using something like SPM for the first time will probably take a little longer that they used to take; this must be allowed for and any potential sufferers of this delay should be warned

• Scope of SPM?
who will use SPM; when; on what type of projects; will every project over two days adopt SPM?

Organise the SPM project
Consider the organisation behind the project:

• nominate a sponsor; make sure the sponsor knows the objectives, the proposed process of implementation and their role in it.

• choose a project manager; consider their credibility (sometimes a project manager from outside the organisation has better credibility).

• identify other interested parties; for example, personnel and training, internal and external customers, sales, marketing, etc.

An outline plan
Here is an outline plan for the implementation of SPM:

• Appoint sponsor, project manager
• Identify target SPM players
• Identify individual implementation opportunities. Don't put a person working

on a very high risk project straight onto SPM for their first project
- Identify individual training needs
- Initiate project management training
- Order SPM copies
- Initiate training
- Implement
- Monitor performance
- Consider the follow-up; SPM clinics, a help desk, a centre of competence

Extra plan for PC tools

If you are going to use a PC to help with the planning process:

- replace/upgrade hardware
- install software
- implement software training
- implement first few projects
- review
- roll out service to other project managers

Monitoring progress

This must be tied very closely to your objectives. There are some simple numerical checks you could carry out:

- does every project over two days have a project definition?
- is every project definition up to date (or, being realistic, no more than three days out of date)?
- does every project over two days have a sponsor and a project manager?

Follow it up

Next step (and this should be handled with a little tact, so as not to appear to be too interrogatory):

- select a project manager who has implemented SPM
- ask to see the Project Definitions
- pick one: ask to be shown the project and see how well the definition reflects what is happening on the project

Review the scope

This only leaves 'other work', and some of this maybe should be

'SPM'd'. Unless your people fill in timesheets (from which large slabs of non-SPM project time can be identified), or you have an encyclopaedic knowledge of their activities, you can only pick up whether they are using SPM on every appropriate opportunity by observation.

Potential problems

Here are some common problems with implementing SPM, together with some suggested fixes:

• Projects are 'too large' for SPM

So what are you using instead? SPM will be better than nothing, even on a large project. There are methodologies around for large projects if you really want to formalise such jobs. Alternatively, see Appendix C for information on 'larger' methods.

• Projects are 'too small' for SPM

Don't use SPM. Make sure that these 'small projects' actually are projects in their own right. Maybe they are tasks from some other, bigger, piece of work, which should be in the system.

• SPM is taking too much time

Yes, it will take longer at first. If it is still taking too long after, say, 10 projects, consider the following:

- **scrap it** — it doesn't fit your environment (but what is so special about your environment?)
- **change personnel** — is your project manager up to it, motivated, committed?
- **review the training** — maybe more coaching or formal training will do it
- **tune SPM** — maybe your environment is such that certain parts of SPM really are too time-consuming.

• Projects still fail

Start collecting honest facts; are your project managers being given enough time and support to do a good job?

• It works in our pilot projects and we want to roll it out, but we have many people to train

Training in SPM is not difficult and there are no copyright problems. So your training people could develop and run the training, thereby cutting costs.

• We started using SPM, but it has now faded out

You must find out why this has happened. This type of fade out is not unique to SPM (remember the fuss and hype over the national quality standard BS5750, BS EN ISO9000). If there are structural or procedural problems with SPM then call for assistance with tuning and re-implementation. Otherwise review your management commitment. If your management is not committed to a methodology such as SPM, how can you expect your project management staff to maintain their commitment?

• Demonstrating management commitment

How can you demonstrate management commitment? Here are some suggestions to help you re-establish the visible management commitment to SPM:

- Insist upon project definitions and sign them off
- Carry out spot checks of project definitions
- Respect their project definitions, even if you have doubts; let them run their projects according to their own project definitions
- Review project definitions during your regular progress meetings
- Use project definitions yourself
- Make project definitions public; get each project manager to post the project definitions on a notice board for all to see.

• We've just merged with XYZ and they use their own project management approach. Should we switch to theirs, or force SPM on them?

Firstly, SPM is unusual in that it is specifically designed for small projects. Are the XYZ people actually using their approach on small projects? Maybe you should be looking at a two-tier approach, with SPM for all small projects and the XYZ method for all larger jobs. If you can prove the business benefits of SPM then you might be able to convince them to switch to SPM.

Proving the business benefits

The business benefits of implementing SPM are:

- control over the mass of small projects that make up the greater part of business life
- facts about progress, risks and achievements
- assurance that the right end product is being produced, to cost and time targets
- early warning of potential problems, with options for dealing with them

Measuring the achievement of these benefits should not be left to a 'How do we feel about this' type of subjective measurement. If you are serious about improving your project management effectiveness you should try to set up some objective measures.

Measuring the benefits

1. Simple measures

• how many people should be using SPM?

• how many people are using SPM?

• how many projects are being managed using SPM (ie, how many have project definition Forms)?

• how many projects also have one or more of the optional forms (Risk Assessment, Change Management Sheet, Project Quality Plan, Project Budget)?

• how many small projects are there that are not controlled by SPM (and why not)?

2. Effectiveness

• Ask senior management

• Do you feel in better control over the mass of small projects you have delegated to project managers?

• Why, or why not

• Are you receiving regular factual progress reports?

• Are the company's projects finishing on time, on budget, meeting business requirements, more often than they used to?

• Are you being warned of potential problems before they occur?

• **Ask project managers**

• Do you feel in control of your portfolio of projects?

• Why or why not?

• Are the overheads of SPM worthwhile?

• Why or why not?

What next?

Congratulations on reaching this far! I am glad that I have been able to keep your interest for all these pages. I hope that you are now mulling over what you should do to implement SPM. The forms in Appendix A are provided copyright free for to you to use as you see fit. They contain the elements which you need to control your small projects effectively.

I believe that there are considerable business benefits to be gained from applying good project management practice. You may well find that as your projects cross that grey borderline between small and large, you will need to adopt more sophisticated tools and techniques. However the basic principles set out here will still hold good as you widen your horizon to explore the world of project management still further.

Appendix A

SPM Forms

SPM1 Project Definition

SPM2 Project Risk Assessment

SPM3 Change Management

SPM4 Budget Plan for Project

SPM5 Project Quality Plan

SPM6 Project Task List

SPM1 **PROJECT DEFINITION**

Project Name and Brief Description

Project Outline

Objectives • What is the project designed to achieve

Scope • What is included, what is excluded

Constraints

Roles and Responsibilities • Project Sponsor, Customer, Manager

Main Products/Deliverables • What is to be produced, in what form

External Dependencies • Links to other projects

Underlying Assumptions

Project Phases/Tasks

Phase/Task	Resource	Start Date	End Date	Status

Project Review Points

Date or Project Event	Review Deliverable	Review Method	Actual Status

Approvals/Authorisation

Project Sponsor	name:	approval to begin: date:	completion: date:
Project Manager			
Project Customer			

	reqd?		reqd?
Risk Assessment		**Project Quality Plan**	
Change Management Sheet		**Project Budget**	

SPM2 PROJECT RISK ASSESSMENT

Project Name and Brief Description

Compiled By: **Date:**

Approved By: **Date:**

Risk:

Preventive Actions:

Contingent Actions:

Trigger Actions:

Risk:

Preventive Actions:

Contingent Actions:

Trigger Actions:

Risk:

Preventive Actions:

Contingent Actions:

Trigger Actions:

Risk:

Preventive Actions:

Contingent Actions:

Trigger Actions:

Risk:

Preventive Actions:

Contingent Actions:

Trigger Actions:

SPM3 CHANGE MANAGEMENT

Project Name and Brief Description

Compiled By: **Date:**

Change:

Implications:

Accepted By: **date:**

Change:

Implications:

Accepted By: **date:**

Change:

Implications:

Accepted By: **date:**

Change:

Implications:

Accepted By: date:

Change:

Implications:

Accepted By: date:

Change:

Implications:

Accepted By: date:

Change:

Implications:

Accepted By: date:

SPM4 BUDGET PLAN FOR PROJECT:

Item																				

Compiled By: Date:

SPM5 **PROJECT QUALITY PLAN**

Project Name and Brief Description

Compiled By: **Date:**

Approved By: **Date:**

Quality Targets:

Prioritised targets against which the success of the project will be judged, e.g. Delivery Date, Development Cost, Quality of Product. The latter must be expressed in specific terms, based upon Functionality, Usability, Reliability, Performance, Serviceability

Accepted By: **Date:**

Approach to be used:

Standards, Methods, Technologies, Tools. Justification of deviation from normal standards.

Implementation Strategy:

Outline of method of implementation, including implications of strategies such as parallel or pilot implementations

Major Products to be Reviewed

Product: target review date:

Review Method:

Findings: actual review date:

Corrective Action Required:

Action Taken By: corrective action date:

Product: target review date:

Review Method:

Findings: actual review date:

Corrective Action Required:

Action Taken By: corrective action date:

SPM6 **PROJECT PHASE/TASK LIST**

Project Name and Brief Description

Project Phases/Tasks

Phase/Task	Resource	Start Date	End Date	Status

Appendix B

SPM Checklists

Checklist 1 • Starting the Project

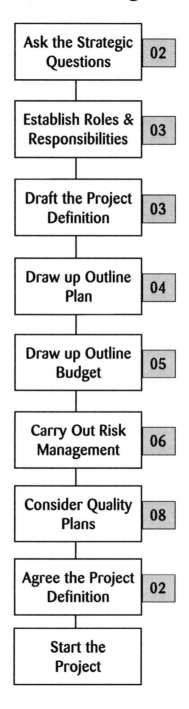

Ask the Strategic Questions — 02

Establish Roles & Responsibilities — 03

Draft the Project Definition — 03

Draw up Outline Plan — 04

Draw up Outline Budget — 05

Carry Out Risk Management — 06

Consider Quality Plans — 08

Agree the Project Definition — 02

Start the Project

Checklist 2 • Running the Project

Measure and Manage Progress	07
Review the Project Definition	02
Verify Quality	08
Manage Changes	09
Deal with Problems	12
Keep Control of the Wider Issues	11
Review and Close the Project	10

00 Indicates the relevant Chapter number

Appendix C

Methods

For large projects there are any number of formal methods that you can choose to use. In the public domain you will find that PRINCE (PRojects IN Controlled Environments) is mandatory for some UK government projects. It is a safe and orderly way to manage a large project.

It has drawbacks, however. It is seen as very cumbersome for 'small' projects, where small means six months or less. It is also perceived as being rather bureaucratic and difficult to tune (difficult to adapt the standard approach to meet the specific conditions of a particular project).

The new version, PRINCE2, is seen as being less prescriptive. To find out more about PRINCE2 contact the CCTA (part of H.M. Treasury in Norwich).

Many organisations do not use PRINCE at all. They run large projects, but do not want the bureaucracy associated with PRINCE. For these environments SPM can be stretched, but it has been designed primarily for small projects.

CCTA: Roseberry Court, St. Andrew's Business Park, Norwich NR7 0HS Tel: 01603 704704

The Relationship between PRINCE and SPM

more than 9 months	Definitely PRINCE
9 months	Maybe PRINCE / Maybe SPM
2 months	
1 month	Definitely SPM
2 days	

Project Manager Today

Project Manager Today Publications specialises in project management and related books and journals. Titles include:

'Managing Smaller Projects'

The International Journal of Project and Business Risk Management
(£240 Corporate subscription; individual to a home address £67.50)

and the flagship monthly magazine:

Project Manager Today
(£29.50 p.a.)

Full details from: Project Manager Today Publications
PO Box 55, Wokingham, Berkshire, RG40 4XN

Project Manager Today is a sponsor of the Spring and Autumn Project Management Exhibitions and organises a range of seminars at the exhibitions and topical conferences and seminars during the year. Full details from:

Jim Potter, Conference and Events Manager,
PO Box 515, Sutton, Surrey SM2 6EN